Tempus ORAL HISTORY *Series*

voices of
Ealing
and Hounslow

Bomb damage at the Glaxo factory, Greenford, 1944.

Tempus ORAL HISTORY *Series*

voices of
Ealing
and Hounslow

Compiled by
Sue McAlpine

First published 2000
Copyright © Sue McAlpine, 2000

Tempus Publishing Limited
The Mill, Brimscombe Port,
Stroud, Gloucestershire, GL5 2QG

ISBN 0 7524 1886 6

Typesetting and origination by
Tempus Publishing Limited
Printed in Great Britain by
Midway Clark Printing, Wiltshire

'Sweet Fanny Adams', 1934. Dick Adams with his father, sister Marjorie, uncle, mother Fanny, aunt, baby and cousin Queenie.

Contents

Acknowledgements

Firstly, and most importantly, I would like to thank all the people who contributed to *Voices of Ealing and Hounslow*. Without their unique memories I would never have had the pleasure of meeting them or the enjoyment in compiling this book.

I am deeply indebted to PlayBack Reminiscence Theatre at the Questors Theatre, Ealing, who have allowed me to use their extraordinary and extensive oral history collection, now deposited at Gunnersbury Park Museum. I am very grateful to Mary Horner for allowing me to use the excerpts from her family memoirs about her father John Hearn and for the Museum of the Order of St John for the use of Fred Sims' memories.

I would especially like to thank Jane Dewey for her stalwart help in setting up the Oral History Archive at Gunnersbury Park Museum and to her, Rachelle Ellis and Shaaron Whetlor for their initial inspiration and guidance. I am very grateful to Doreen McDermott and John Cordon for their marvellous help and also to Margaret Philips, Carla Field, Gillian Shortt and Eileen Humphries for hours of interviewing, editing and transcribing. Vera Burrows has invariably and patiently provided me with memories whenever I asked her and Dick Adams generously allowed me to raid his family photograph albums. I would also like to thank Christine Garland of PlayBack and Carolyn Hammond of Chiswick Library for their help and advice, and my youngest daughter, Jessie, for helping me with typing.

The majority of the photographs in the book belong personally to the contributors and I am very grateful to them for allowing me to use them. Some of the photographs have been taken from the collections at the Local History Library, London Borough of Ealing and from Gunnersbury Park Museum and Chiswick Local Studies Library, for which I thank CIP, working in partnership with the London Borough of Hounslow.

I am most grateful to Gill Mathias for allowing me to use her own photographs on pages: 63 and 111; also to Canal+ Image UK Ltd for permission to use the Ealing Studios photographs on pages 35, 45, 46, 47 and 48; to Mirror Syndication International for page 82 (bottom); and to Marks and Spencer Company Archive for page 110.

Introduction

When I first started working at Gunnersbury Park Museum, the local history museum for the London Boroughs of Ealing and Hounslow, I listened to many local people talking about their lives: the good times and the bad times. As we began to record these memories and make them part of the museum's collection, we realised not only that they were a fascinating source of social history, invaluable for future generations, but as a whole gave an extraordinarily vivid picture of twentieth-century life. This book gives you a taste of some of the wonderful memories we collected and are continuing to gather.

My first encounter was with the women who had worked before and after the war in the tin shop at Chiswick's Cherry Blossom Shoe Factory, some straight after leaving Hogarth School at fourteen. It was not long before voices were raised as the floodgates opened and out poured the memories, each participant vying with the other for juicier reminiscences. The coup de grace was when Stan, then well into his seventies, walked into the room. There was a stunned silence, followed by some suppressed giggling. It turned out that the Cherry Blossom women had not seen him since he worked there as the van boy in the early thirties. If you look at his photograph on page 44 you'll understand why they all fancied him! I subsequently invited the ladies back to meet the current children of Hogarth School; the roars of laughter between the two generations, as they swapped school experiences, were pure delight!

Since then, with the help of skilled and committed oral history volunteers, we have collected hundreds of memories, across a range of experiences. They now form part of the museum archive and some of them are now published in book form for the first time. There are memories here that go back to the early part of the last century. Ada Banks was 102 when we first recorded her memories. She remembered Zeppelins and castor oil tablets in her tin bath in front of the kitchen range; Noel Richmond Watson remembered his father riding up Horsenden Hill to shout the all clear during the First World War.

We are given a poignant insight into the hard times of the 1930s, the days of the pawnbroker and the tallyman, gas lighting and shared washing facilities. There are childhood memories: playing in the streets, fag card game and tin can copper. There are memories of shopping in Goodbans in Chiswick or Sayers in Ealing or going to the Chiswick Empire to throw nuts and orange peel at the 'posh people' below. There are sad memories such as Tommy Osborne's devastating description of his mother's death in the Brentford Canal and Julius Fletcher's escape from Nazi Germany, within months of the outbreak of the war. There are extraordinary memories such as John Hearn's brush with death when he jumped off the tailgate of a lorry with an unexploded bomb under each arm. There are the unusual memories of filming the old Ealing comedies at the Ealing film studios. Ajit Rai's sensitive descriptions of the Southall riots and of bussing children out of the area are deeply disturbing.

For me there have been some special moments. I shall never forget laughing with Cissy Randall when she described her father chasing her sister's boyfriend down the road with the copper stick. I have enjoyed chatting with Vera Burrows who has told me so much about her life, pulling out memories like a rabbit from a hat. All I needed to say was, 'Oh, Vera, do you remember...?' and she'd be off! Fred Sims gripped us all, adults and children alike, with a mixture of laughter and tears as he recalled his extraordinary memories of life in a German prisoner of war camp during the Second World War. I'll always remember when Andrea Cameron, Hounslow's very eminent and much respected local history librarian, was prompted, by the sound of rock and roll emanating from a fifties Wurlitzer, to tell the story of her teenage net petticoats. They were hidden from her disapproving mother in a paper bag and changed into, in the ladies' at Hammersmith Palais.

The reminiscences brought together in this book cover many different experiences. Perhaps the most shocking are the stories of those people who came to Britain from other countries, particularly from India and Pakistan, from the West Indies and from Uganda. Their frank and honest testimonies of the difficulties they faced when they first came to this country give us a penetrating insight of those times. They are an important part of the history of this country and tell us much about the relationships between one culture and another. They make us think how much or perhaps how little, things have changed since then.

And so our archive has grown. However, it is with the generous and longsighted decision of PlayBack Reminiscence Theatre at Questors Theatre, Ealing, who very kindly agreed to deposit their extraordinary and extensive oral history collection at the museum that has made it such a rich and unique collection. Over many years PlayBack has recorded memories of hundreds of people living and working in Ealing, written original plays performed at Questors Theatre and on tour, and given so many older people in the community huge enjoyment and a sense of pride and achievement in their lives. Many of these memories are now published in this book. They include the laundry workers of Acton's Soapsud Island, the orphaned children of Hanwell's Cuckoo School, where Charlie Chaplin was sent for a short time as a child, as well as the fascinating and unusual memories of some of the people who worked at Ealing Film Studios.

Sometimes memories need jogging, but once the ball is rolling, they flow with immediacy and spontaneity, even from those who insist they have nothing to offer or say they can remember little. There is really no such thing as an 'ordinary' memory. On the contrary they are all of unique value, recalling a time and place that no longer exists, bringing the past alive in a way that no history book can do. All the contributors to this book and to the archive should feel proud of themselves; by sharing with us their personal memories, they have greatly enriched our understanding of the past.

I would like to think that those people who gave their memories enjoyed the telling as much as I did the listening. It has been such a pleasure for me to listen and meet so many people. I can only add that I strongly feel it is vital to catch and bottle the memories before the past fades and vanishes altogether. So, why not start by recording the older members of your family or, perhaps more to the point, insist that somebody hears what you have to say?

CHAPTER 1
Childhood

Edna Cox, 1920.

Castor Oil

My mother had Tom, Will, Jack, me, Alice, Sue, and Charlie. There were ten children in all and never one of us had to have a doctor. Mother used to bathe us every Friday night and she used to give us a tablet. We learned what it was after a time. She used to give it to us when she was scrubbing us in the bath, you know and that, and this 'ere tablet used to be melting and melting, you know, and I realized it was a castor oil tablet. That was the only way she could give it to us. I was a slave in them days, used to do all the dirty work for Mother.

Ada Banks

Cowboys and Indians: Dick Adams and Raymond Gardener in Lancaster Road, off Bakers Lane, Ealing, 1928.

Bath Time

Friday night was treat night. You had syrup of figs in the bath in front of the fire. And that was a regular routine. Everybody, Friday night, had syrup of figs and the bath in front of the fire. The water came from an old big copper, which was in the scullery in those days. You just boiled the water in this copper and brought it out in a ladle and put it in the bath.

Ruby Pays

The Stink Pipe

Most of the games we played were things like cigarette cards, flick 'em up against the wall and whoever got nearest won. Or we stood one up against a wall and you had to hit it. Other things in those days was of course the yo-yo and the biff bat, which was like a piece of table tennis bat with a hole in the middle and a piece of rubber with a ball on the end. Also the looperoo which was a spinning rope like a cowboy's. Several of us had Meccano sets and we would make models and go up to the end of the alley, shelter it off and charge kids cigarette cards to look at the models working. Bakers Lane was very narrow and was the best place to go roller skating. There was the stink pipe in Wells Place. It was a pipe about thirty foot high which took the smells from the sewers below. It was a well known meeting place: 'See you round the stink pipe'.

Dick Adams

Gas Lighting

I can remember the house when it was gas lit, and I can remember it eventually being wired for electric light. We only had one power socket, which was for the radio. I remember the gas mantles, the filament which glows when the gas is lit – very delicate, you had to extract them very carefully when you wanted to change them, from a very small cardboard box you got from the local grocer's shop. The light actually was very yellow but that's what we had and that's what we liked at the time. There was a light in every room including the scullery but there wasn't one in the small bedroom and that one, like the outside loo, had to make do with an oil lamp. When the electric lights were installed, in 1936, this was only done in the main room; the scullery was still gas lit. All the gas and the electric was by coin slot. I think it was a shilling in the slot at the time, so you always had to make sure you had some in the house.

Frank Weeden

Milkman's Boy

Round the corner from us was a large Co-op dairy. Horse and cart milk delivery that went to Northolt, Greenford, Perivale and parts of Hanwell and Southall. They must have had about thirty horses. I can remember being fascinated by them as a child. The dairy was next to a Salvation Army hall and you could climb up the wall and look over into the yard where the horses were stabled and you could see the blacksmith and the horses being shod. During the war my sister had a boyfriend called Dick Plum, a name you're not likely to forget! He was about seventeen, waiting to be called up, so I asked him if I could be his milk boy. It was not really allowed – we would meet the milkman just a little way down the road. They were not supposed to have children working on the vans, but they all

At the Brentham Estate, Ealing.

did, they all had their milkman's boy, paid out of their own pockets. Dick had this round which went to Northolt, and this horse called Mary, a sort of chestnut mare with black legs, a black mane and a black tail – a beautiful animal. You could cuddle her and kiss her and I used to take apples and let the horse eat it from my mouth. The round used to start in Costons Lane in Greenford. The horse always knew the round and would stop at the right places, especially where someone would come out and give them a treat, an apple here, a piece of bread there, a bucket of water somewhere else. It would move on up until it got outside the house and actually mount the pavement and put its head over the gate, waiting for the person to come out.

John Cordon

Scarlet Fever

When I was about six years old I contracted scarlet fever. This was in 1909. My mother and father wanted me to take a dose of castor oil. My dad said to me, 'You take a dose of castor oil when you come out of hospital and you'll find sixpence on the mantelpiece.' But when I came out after six weeks there was no sixpence; he'd bribed me. I was carted off to Clayponds Fever Hospital. My mother and father used to come and visit me on a Sunday, but they weren't allowed into the room I was in. All they could do was to stand outside and mouth at me and try to make me understand what they were saying.

Bill Axbey

May Day

May Day processions took place in the borough. Weeks before, there was a frenzy of activity, Mum making dresses for my sister and me, white and frilly, together with a band decorated with artificial flowers to go round our heads. We also carried poles decorated with flowers. On the great day the younger children were put into the decorated coal carts, still smelling of coal, and the older children formed a procession and the whole lot set off around the streets, finishing at Brentham Institute for maypole dancing. Presumably a May Queen was in attendance but I was too busy enjoying myself to notice.

Doreen McDermott

Escape from Germany

I was twelve in 1933, when Hitler came to power. I remember it was turmoil. There were people getting hurt, people walking with their flags through the streets and being attacked by the Brownshirts, the brown troopers, before the Nazi party was officially in government. It was devastating: we used to write to our relatives abroad and they couldn't understand how much it was affecting our life. It was a terrible time. A nightmare, I can't describe it as anything else. You found yourself in a dilemma – every German was made to salute this flag of the swastika, but we as Jews were not allowed to do that, so consequently if a group with a banner-carrying person walked along the road and you stood at the kerb, you were not as a Jew supposed to salute the

May Day 1936. Doreen McDermott is second from the right, next to her younger sister, Brenda.

flag. Some people did, simply to hide their identity, but I... if I stood there without raising my arm, people immediately identified me as a Jew. So we had this terrible dilemma. If we were identified as a Jew, for no reason they attacked you.

The headmaster decided that life in Germany by that time had become impossible and he managed to get somebody to guarantee our stay in England for the next two years. It was done at a very short notice and I was one of the first twelve boys to come to England. We were seeking this Major Davidson who was supposed to be the guarantor. We later – after the war – discovered that this Major Davidson didn't exist; it was just a means of getting us out of Germany in May 1939, barely four months before the Second World War started. We came over in the 'children transport' – we were on our own, twelve eighteen-year-old boys. We went by train along the Rhine and eventually to Hook of Holland where we boarded the ship to Harwich. We arrived in Harwich the morning of 4 May 1939. I still remember the first time I saw a flying boat in the bay. We took a train to Liverpool Street station and I was devastated, I can't call it anything else, to go through these black tunnels, simply a black hole. That was my first taste of London. What made it worse was that we were waiting on the platform for somebody to meet us and when they came they said, 'Oh, we've got a wonderful place for you but you've got to go by tram.' So we went from Liverpool Street to Mansell Street, near Aldgate East station. It was called the shelter, a place for people without homes, or refugees like ourselves but we discovered then that the shelter was full, there wasn't enough room. 'Oh,' they said, 'we've got a wonderful place for you round the corner in Whitechapel in the Mile End

Road.' We walked to this wonderful place and it turned out to be Rowton House in the East End of London. I still remember we didn't sleep at all, it was dirty, with bugs, a terrible place. Eventually I found a really nice place: it was a hostel for young sailors that came to the Pool of London and this was the only place in the East End which had its own swimming pool and billiard table. We were there for three weeks till I managed to find a job as an engineer. I became a toolmaker in Hanwell with a firm called Andrew Frazer.

Julius Fletcher

Indoor Toilet

Mother used to take in washing from people. She also used to go out cleaning houses, some of the big houses up The Grove. I remember Miss Willoughby at No. 12. There was something I thought was unusual – the lavatory was actually inside the house! You didn't have to go out in the garden for it. I thought it was most unsanitary. Fancy having a toilet in the house!

Dick Adams

Secret Places

Our houses were back-to-back; the streets made a square so we called it 'playing round the block' – Cowboys and Indians, It. We made carts of pram wheels and planks: some of them were quite elaborate, we even had brakes on. Another favourite was marbles, played in the gutter, and cigarette cards. We collected these from the adults, who all smoked of course. Fag-card game was done by standing a card against the wall and your opponent started flicking cards against it. You joined in as well and a lot of them missed and just laid about on the ground and were left to lie on the ground until somebody knocked down the target card. The one who knocked down the target card picked up all the cards that were on the ground. He then set up another and so the game went on. We had secret places in the brick walls, which we whittled out by raking out the mortar. In this we hid our favourites – marbles, pennies, conkers.

Frank Weeden

Battery Acid

The entertainment at the time was the wireless. It ran off a huge dry battery that lasted three months, and two wet accumulators. They only lasted a week, and it was my job on a Saturday morning to get them recharged, which meant carrying them through Acton Green to Turnham Green Terrace where there was a shop which recharged accumulators. They had an open top with very strong acid in them and they were quite dangerous, really. The wireless wouldn't work without them. One day I was going too fast and I spilled some of the acid. It ruined a pair of trousers which was a major tragedy. From as early as I can remember we listened to the wireless. During the war it was fantastic: lots of news, no doubt a lot of propaganda. I remember listening to Lord Haw Haw, the traitor who broadcast from Germany. Funny voice, we laughed at him; the things he said we knew weren't true and so it was just like a comedy show. It was a great morale builder. Churchill's speeches for instance – some of the great moments of this century. The thing I remember as a child, of course, was *Children's Hour*. I used to rush home to listen to it from school. They were so intelligent and entertaining. There were the comedy plays, *Toy Town* with Mr Growser and Dennis the Dachshund and the Policeman and Mr Mayor and Larry the Lamb, of course played by Uncle Mac. The presenters of *Children's Hour* were either aunties or uncles. Uncle Mac and Uncle David I remember most. Derek McCulloch. Then there was *The Boy Detectives*, I remember. It annoyed me because the boys were played by girls and I could never understand why. There was *Jennings at School*, and *Said the Cat to the Dog* was one of the series about Monty the cat and Peckham the dog. *Cowley's Farm* was a nature programme and introduced you to farming and country matters, quite foreign to anybody who lived in London. *Children's Hour* was an absolutely fantastic programme. Then I remember the comedy programmes in the evening. Never thought much of Arthur Askey, though he was quite popular; there was Tommy Handley with *ITMA* – 'It's That Man Again' – which was a sort of nonsense thing. *Much Binding in the Marsh* I think was my favourite, with Kenneth Horn and Richard Murdoch.

John Rogers

Family Favourites

My father used to like the radio and bought each new addition. He had one with a special facility, band spreading. You could tune in roughly to a station then fine tune with another knob. We used to have an aerial right to the end of the garden. *Family Favourites* were Monday night at 8 p.m. In this programme was a deliberate mistake: it

Edna Razzelle at Cliftonville in the early 1930s.

was fun trying to spot it. Sid Walker, he used to tell a tale of mystery. We used to listen to the radio in the dining room, the front room was only used on special occasions. My sister loved *The Ovaltinies*. Saturday night was bath night. We would sit round the fire and listen to *Saturday Night Music Hall* with Henry Hall. That was the highlight of the week.

John Cordon

Chaperoning

In those days we were segregated, even for something like badminton. The girls played first and then they were ushered off the premises and the boys were allowed in. If you appeared in the wrong group you'd probably have to go home, accompanied by an adult. Even when I went to play tennis I was chaperoned.

Edna Razzelle

Acton Hospital

Our doctor was Dr Chate in Gunnersbury Lane. I remember once at football I had a sprain. I had to cut the boot off and hobble home. Chate came down and made me walk on it straight away: 'It's not a break, just get up and walk on it'. My sisters were disgusted with Chate. When they had a cold he would say, 'Look, all you've got is a bit of ribbon between you and the whole of creation. Go and put something on!' My brother broke his arm birds-nesting over Gunnersbury Park. He was chased away by one of the keepers and ran all the way to Acton Hospital. He daren't tell Mother and told the hospital some sort of fib and they set his arm. That was 1932. I played football over Gunnersbury Park, was smashed across the nostrils and was sent off practically blind. I went straight up to Acton Hospital where they straightened my nose. At wintertime we used to go to the Chiswick Empire about six in the evening, especially Mondays. If any of the acts wanted youngsters planted in the audience, they'd be taken on at the stage door. You had to be in the audience so you saw all the acts. You were paid sixpence at the end of the week on Sunday to make sure you turned up during the week. I've been on the stage at Chiswick trying to ride a unicycle and falling off. Never needed the hospital for that though!

Dennis Bowen

Paradise Alley

All the children played at the top of the alley. On frosty mornings we made lovely slides – they steamrolled the tarmac and it froze beautifully. A running jump and off we went, brilliant. We had whips and tops – we used to really belt them one, for yards up the road, spinning all the time. I'd keep mine going all the way to school, St Paul's School down the road. We used to pay tin can copper; you had a tin and you put a stone in it so you could rattle it, bashed in so it didn't come out. One person stood in the middle of the road and you all went to hide and then you came out and you were supposed to catch the person; when you caught somebody you banged the can on the ground. Then there was kiss chase, with your secret, you know, somebody that was sweet on you, or somebody you liked. You all ran and hid and then you chased somebody and when you caught them, you gave them a kiss. Then there was bung the barrel, like leapfrogging on top of everybody, but you always finished up in a heap on the floor. Fag cards, you used to line them up on the pavement and flick them down. When anybody came out of the tobacco shop you'd rush up and say, 'Can we have your fag cards, Mister?' We used to ride down the hill at Albany Road on our barrow made out a piece of wood, a rope and some old pram wheels. You'd sit on the barrow with your feet on the two front wheels while the person would run and push you and then jump on the back

I used to save pennies, I've always been a one for saving money here and there. I had a firework club and a Christmas club, so that I could buy a Christmas present for Mum and Dad, just a bar of chocolate or something. In the little sweet shop, I'd give her halfpence and she used to put it down on a card. I'd save about two shillings. If I didn't put anything in the Christmas club then I'd put it in the fireworks club. My mother used to like a drop of Guinness so I had to go down to the Albany Arms with a jug. Children weren't allowed in the public bar so I went into the Jug and Bottle part. I didn't mind doing that, as long as I didn't drop it. That was more than my life was worth!

Vera Burrows

Photographed by the Lavatory

My father had a camera, a Brownie 620. It came from Durbin's the chemist. My father used to clean the windows there, well he cleaned virtually all the windows in the area. This camera had been dropped and got bent. it was 21s, quite expensive – this was before the war – but they gave it to him for 15s. I used to borrow it: it had three lenses, for landscapes, groups at middle distance and close ups; you just pushed a lever. We always used to have our pictures taken by the lavatory in the garden, probably because it was the sunniest place!

Dick Adams

Saturdays at the Pictures

I went to Sunday School at St Barnabas'. We used to go on outings, we went to

Dick Adams with his grandfather by the outside lavatory, 1927.

the Town Hall and arranged for Coronation mugs and spoons for everybody. I've still got mine.

Doreen McDermott

Long Trousers and Macaroons

I was nine when we came to Ealing, in May 1941. No bananas, no sweets, clothes rationing. Most children were evacuated but there were a few families left, including one chap with a brother and sister. One Sunday he appeared in church in long trousers and I flew into a terrible rage and went home to my parents and said, 'I must have long trousers by next Sunday!' Clothing was rationed, so they sorted round a few coupons and got me some long trousers. So my pride was reconstructed. After the war I became a telegram boy, that was at Christmas to earn a bit of money. And they said 'Can you ride a motorcycle?' and I said 'Yes!' Went outside and in the alleyway I learnt to ride a Pease Bantum in about ten minutes and started delivering telegrams. Zita's coffee house was very posh. My mother used to take me there to have macaroons and coffee sometimes. If you put a fork in them they burst like a grenade and went all over everybody. Lyon's Corner House is where us kids used to go on a Sunday night and chat. If you were quick at the cinema you used to know how to get in at the side door or one of you would pay to go in – ninepence – and then go and open the fire exit so that all your mates could troop in.

Geoff Harper

Burnham beaches where we were let loose, running up and down a huge, huge hole. When I went back recently I was so surprised to see that it was really a tiddly little dip! Every Saturday morning, my father used to take us all down to the Odeon. All the kids in the street, a little maggot of children. He'd buy us all an ice cream. He'd sit and watch too, he loved it. *Crash Currigan, Mickey Mouse, Pluto,* all the old favourites. In 1937 he arranged a street party for the Coronation, in Fowler's Walk. The street was closed for traffic, not that there was much, and all laid out with tables and trestles. The mums dished out all the food. He went to

Hooky

We used the Park a lot. Sometimes the games bordered on what might be now considered hooliganism and we often incurred the wrath of the Park Keeper who chased us. The most feared one we knew as 'Hooky' because he had a hook instead of a forearm and hand. He often brandished this at us.

Frank Weeden

Muddy Lanes and Tram Tracks

When I was a little girl, Gunnersbury Lane was extremely muddy; we didn't often go there because it was a long way for a small child to walk from Walpole Gardens. We used to be taken up the lane, we climbed up the grassy bank at the side and were lifted up to see over the hedge and see the cows. When I think of cows in Chiswick now it makes me sad. The lane itself was a narrow little muddy lane, nothing much to it. If you looked out west at the end of what was the high road you just saw Market Gardens. There was no big road going out west at all, it was endless market gardens. When I was very small, trolleybuses were lovely. Apart from anything else they got rid of the rails which had been quite dangerous for bicycles and quite a lot of people had fallen off by getting their wheels in the tram tracks. The trolleybuses were absolutely beautiful, very smooth and very quiet and you could sit by the driver in the front seat; that was the best thing of all. Of course the buses were a very different cup of tea because they had open tops and sort of canvas sheets which were hooked to the seat in front and when it rained hard you'd get a puddle of water in

your lap. You had to be very careful when you put it down that you didn't get it all over your feet.

Gwyneth Cole

Sharing

I shared a bedroom with my three elder brothers. Three brothers in one bed, and me at the foot and a valence over the bottom, you know these iron bedsteads, and the valence and my little bed at the bottom. I knew what a man looked like before ever I knew anything, because pyjamas were never

Gwyneth Cole, aged three, with her brother Michael, 1924.

19

heard of. My brothers had to step over one another to get to bed. We all shared the same room but there was never anything amiss. Never.

Elizabeth Wilkinson

The Best Years

When I was a child we used to go on the bomb sites and we used to take lots of paraffin and some potatoes and make a bonfire and cook the potatoes. We used to play in the air-raid shelters and that. Also just after the war, I must have been eight or nine, they were bringing all the tanks back from Germany and we used to play on the tanks and things like that. We used to play down the river, by St Nicholas' church, down on all the mud by the slipway there. You used to find lots of bits of clay pipe. I reckon you'd still find bits if you went looking down there. We used to play in Chiswick House Park; the house was derelict then. My gran had a pub in Devonshire Road, Chiswick. It was called the Prince of Wales and they nicknamed it during the war 'The War Office' because of the black market. People used to swap their ration books for drink. We never really went short of much in them days. When I was a small boy in my gran's pub, we had sheds where they stored all the beer at the back of the pub, and I was toddling round there and I fell over and cut my head open which gave me a big scar. When they used to stitch things up, there wasn't a lot done, so they just put pepper on it to dry the blood up. I had this scar on my face and when I was at school they used to call me Scarface and that. When I was a teenager everyone thought I was a villain so people didn't pick on me; having a scar on my face was really to my advantage. I was mad on motorbikes, like all teenagers, and I used to go to the Ace Café on the North Circular where all the rockers used to go. In my teenage days I used to go to all the local dance halls, like the Palais and the Boathouse at Kew, that was famous. It was good, teenage years, I think they were the best years. In fact I think I've lived through the best years. I would live my life over again any time!

David Read

Hearthstone

I was the little mum, always the little mum. I had to look after the others and I had to work hard in the house. We used to scrub the street front you know, the path, from the street door down to the gate. The front bit was hearth-stoned, whitened, then you washed the concrete up to the portion under the porch, and then you'd whiten that. You dip the hearthstone in the bucket and rub it over. You'd smooth it beautifully, straight strokes. Mrs Prince, who lived four doors down, she used to come along and see me on my knees there. 'That's right Lizzie, she used to say. 'You do all the corners dear, and the middle will look after itself'.

Elizabeth Wilkinson

CHAPTER 2

Schooldays

The woodwork shop at the Central London District School in Hanwell. It was known as the Cuckoo School and took in orphaned children from all over London. Charlie Chaplin was there for a short time in the 1920s.

No Visitors

I was at the Cuckoo School in Hanwell from 1922 to 1932. I went there when I was three years old. I got this message from my mother's sister. What happened was that I was the youngest of five boys, and being poor they took the youngest one away and it was me. It's as simple as that. It was no account of me being a bastard or anything like that – forget that. It was a case of being under the Poor Law and coming from Bermondsey, in the Old Kent Road. I was taken away. I never used to get visitors and one day a kid came and he

The Cuckoo School buildings.

said, 'Hey you've got some visitors', well I said 'No one comes to see me', and I wouldn't go. And one of the Officers, he says, 'Gillies, you come here, visiting room – you've got some visitors.' There was no one in the visiting room. I went and tapped on the caretaker's door and I went in and I said, 'Mr Holmes, Mr Squires said I had to come in here.' He said 'Yes, there's your mother here.' I looked and I said 'Who?' I didn't know her. I didn't want to either.

Fred Gillies

Red as a Beetroot

I was in the dining hall one day and I was flicking something to one of the other lads. All of a sudden my name got shouted out: 'Stand at the end of the table'. Now what used to happen was this. One side of the large dining hall was the boys – all the boys – and the other side were the girls and there was a six foot gangway in between. You had to stand at the end of the table, right at the end, and you can imagine how I felt standing up there trying to eat my food and about eight hundred boys and girls all staring at me. I remember I was as red as a beetroot.

Arthur Tyson

Gobstoppers

On Saturday we were allowed out of the school. We had pocket money given to us and we'd go down to the sweet shop and buy gobstoppers and threepenny slabs of toffee. You used to get these lovely little liquorice dips, sherbet and bullseyes. I used to have threepence halfpenny a week and I always used to save a ha'penny. Always. In a little box I kept it in. I still do. I feel guilty if I spend money.

Vera Akhurst

Leaving the Cuckoo School

When you left you got a tin trunk of clothes. They made me a dark green costume. I hated it. I was always too busty. I had morning dresses with pinafores and a black afternoon dress and frilly apron, undies and everything, brush and comb and Bible.... oh, and stockings and a dozen diapers [sanitary towels], though I didn't need them yet. I think it was April 1922.

Alice Pearce

Floors like Glass

The first thing I can remember was when my sister took me to Westmoreland Road Workhouse. Later I saw my mother, I think it was, in bed in hospital. She took some earrings and put them in my ears, old-fashioned turquoise ones. My sister took the earrings out of my ears and left me in the workhouse. After a month they took me to Hanwell School, in Ealing. When I got there, the first thing was to see a doctor, have all your hair shaved off, like a boy, and your teeth seen to. I went out into the hall and saw these two people there who was me sister and brother. I didn't really know them because it seemed a long while since I'd seen them. I never knew me father and mother – must have been that lady who died then and there.

The dining hall of the Cuckoo School, 1931.

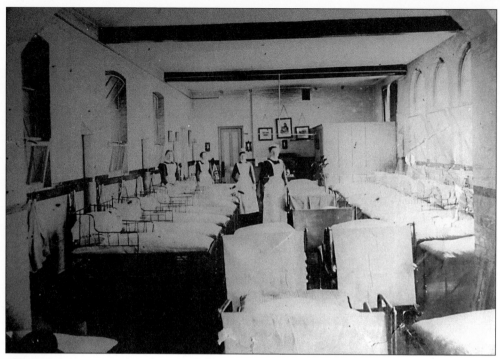

The dormitory.

Now, you had to go to bed at six o'clock at night and get up at six in the morning. In the morning when you got up, shivering and cold, you had to fold your blankets and sheets all in proper neat piles. The nurse used to put polish all down that ward and then twelve of us at a time had to get on our hands and knees and, with a cloth on your hand like that, she'd say, 'Ready: one, two, three, go!' and then you had to go down all the ward like that, cleaning and turn at the bottom and all go back. But believe me, those floors were like glass. It taught you to be clean. And then at night you had to undo all that bundle again and make your bed before you got in it – every day of your life!

When you were fourteen, you'd never believe it, for a birthday present, what did they give you? Two sanitary towels. I'm going to tell you honestly, it was just two pieces where the sewing girls had to put a loop on each and a piece of tape and that had to last you. You had to wash it. You had to try and dry them on the pipes.

Lilian Lynford

Baked Spuds

Underneath the gymnasiums there used to be a boiler. If we managed to get hold of some spuds (we pinched them down the farm), we used to force the door on there, we was pretty good at that, put all the spuds underneath, go back there after tea and the spuds was all black, stinking and brown. Just knock the back off and you got baked spuds.

Fred Gillies

Wallop

I couldn't go in the Army because I was deaf in one ear. I was struck by a teacher when I was aged eight. A teacher had to take two classes so we was squashed in three or four to a seat. First lesson was dictation. I asked Bunny what a word was third line down on the blackboard but Bunny was short sighted so he couldn't see and was going to ask me the same thing, so we laughed. The master asked why we was laughing and I said I couldn't read it and it looked like a bad word to me, and wallop on the back of the neck. The teacher was six foot four with hands like an octopus. My ear spurted blood three seats away. I fainted on the floor and was taken to the infirmary.

Fred Shaw

Dishing out the Punishments

Captain Hindnum would announce with the aid of a megaphone the names of the boys that were to receive punishment on Friday. All the lads had to report to him and the rest of the school were called on to parade and marched up to the gymnasium. We were formed in ranks around the hall so that we all faced the front where there was a long table. The lads for punishment were lined up behind the table facing the rest of the school. Captain Hindnum would then call out a name followed by the charge and then ask if they were guilty. You would never dare say you were innocent as that would make the Captain look a fool, and he would punish you just the same. All the punishments would always at least end with a caning. They would make the boys

Cuckoo School boys.

The Cuckoo School Infants' Band.

bend over the table face downwards and the senior boys would fasten straps to the lads' ankles, another of the senior boys would pull their sweater over their heads, while another one would pull up their shorts so that they were very tight. For more serious charges they would get the birch. Straps were used to fasten them down before getting three strokes, after which they had to be taken to the infirmary for treatment. Captain Hindnum was a large man and some of the younger boys would faint when they saw him dishing out punishments.

Ted Tamplin

The Band

One of the best things that ever happened to me at that school was that they taught me music. The bandmaster, his name was Mr Perks. Used to get a few cuffs off his baton, but nothing really hard. I used to play the E flat clarinet. Just a few of the lads I remember in the band: Ginger Jennings used to play the oboe. Bolton used to play the cornet. Larden the euphonium, Benfield the big drum, Taylor the piccolo. 'Cos as you know, a piccolo and an E flat clarinet are compatible. If you don't know, they are. They're the same pitch. I'll always remember when I was learning, if I lost my place, I used to keep half an eye on Taylor and if he took the piccolo away from this lips, I used to drop the clarinet and he used to put his piccolo straight back up. Ah, he was a bugger, he used to keep me going.

Fred Gillies

Hogarth School

The girls' school was one side of Duke's Avenue and the boys the other side so, yes, we were completely divided, not allowed to mix, so to speak. They had a hall built on in the girls' school, at the end of the playground, and if you got behind there, you got bunked up and you climbed to the top of the wall and you could call to the boys over the wall. I'm hanging over the wall nagging at the boys from that angle, there were several of us, and a teacher called Miss Tremble whipped us all on our bottoms and we were sent straight up to Miss Dear and we had to sit outside in the corridor because that was our punishment.

Doris Sands

The Strap

I was at Hogarth till I was fourteen. Miss Irvin was a short, fat lady. She was

Doris Sands at Beverley Infants' School, Harvest Festival 1927. She is the tall one at the back holding the cucumber.

Miss Irvin's class, Hogarth School, 1930. Stan Whetlor is in the third row from the front, second on the left.

Hogarth School football team, 1933/34. Most of these boys were later killed in the Second World War.

smashing. She must have strapped every one of these boys.

Stan Whetlor

The Cruelty Inspector

The only school I ever got a chance to go to was the barge school at Brentford, moored up at the top end of the meadow, in the water still in those days. Used to step off the boat, walk up a bit, and we were at school, in the school barge, see. But mainly I been at work since I was seven or eight years old, winding the paddles and opening the lock gates.

Dad nearly got nicked once up at Watford, because I was drawing a lock paddle under age. This woman was watching me Dad, and we later found out she was an inspector travelling round the canals to see what the kids done, like. She comes down to my Dad and says, 'That boy...' and my Dad says, 'Yeah?' and she says 'How old is he?' 'Well now, he's going on seven.' 'I could nick you for that. He should be at school.' But there was only the barge at Brentford – the town schools wouldn't have us. But nearly all the boat children were helping to get the boats through, helping to make a living. Poor little buggers weren't getting anything out of it, a few sweets now and again, but they was doin' the work that they's told they gotta do. You had to be very careful round the Watford area, that woman was always hanging about. She really used to lay it into yer. 'If I see them winding up these sluices under age again, I'll have you for it.' Dad used to say, 'No use arguing with that silly old git,' and my Mum used to say, 'Joe, now listen: you can't argue with them people. She's a cruelty inspector and what they're doing, winding up paddles and opening them heavy gates, she's got that down as cruelty.' I used to like school and I would have preferred to have gone to school than be messed about like I was messed about.

Tommy Osborne

Infants' School

I started school when I was four; that would have been 1926. I went to the Rothschild Infants' School. It was made of tin. They were quite strict. We had slates and slate pencils. There was a coke stove in the middle of the classroom.

Mary Huxley

Left-handed

I started at the age of five at Lammas School. I remember the outdoor toilets and the smell of the school, a smell sort of like creosote. And there were long dark corridors. I was left-handed and, all for the best in those days, they tied my left hand behind my back. The prize each week for the child with the best handwriting was to play the drums in the school orchestra. Needless to say, I never got to play the drums but I think they felt so sorry for me that they let me play the triangle.

Josie Breslauer

School Milk

I remember free milk at school, which came in short stocky quarter-pint bottles, capped

Boat children before the First World War.

The boatman's school in 1955.

was in the class of Mr Woodward to prepare for the eleven-plus exam. He was a superb teacher. He was strict but everybody loved him and I never came across another teacher like him. He had migraines and occasionally went sick and they tried to bring in replacement teachers. And nobody could handle the class – South Acton was a very rough area, it was a very rough class. Mr Woodward, or Woody as we called him, had us strongly under control but anybody else coming in – no hope. There were thirty to forty children in the class. After a few minutes we would get fed up with the new replacement teacher and we didn't understand, we didn't know where Woody was but we knew we wanted him back. You ended up with the whole class slamming their desks lids in unison shouting 'we want Woody, we want Woody.'

John Rogers

The Street Playground

with a cardboard disc. They had a part-cut centre section, which you could put a straw in; it was always a risky thing because you usually squirted milk in your eyes. I never enjoyed it because it was always rather sickly and warm as they stacked the crates near the radiator.

Frank Weeden

Woody

At nine years old, after several schools due to evacuation and moving around, I started at Rothschild Road School where I

My sister went to the Joseph Lancaster School, which shut in 1925. The playground at the back was only for the young children and the boys. The senior girls had to come out and play in the road right in front of our house. When it was cold my sister used to come in and have a cup of tea. There was no traffic except sometimes Harris the butcher who was rather a mad driver. He had a two-wheeled van and he used to come down that road with his horse and whiz round the corner. I can never understand how he didn't hit anybody.

Dick Adams

Bussing out of Southall

When our children started going to school, the host community parents resented it. They said, 'These black children are bringing down the standard of our children,' so then they started protesting against the admission of our children. Mr Boyd, he was in the Tory government, he came down to Southall to listen to the host community parents. He said no more than thirty per cent 'blackies' be admitted into the schools. Then the bussing started. Our children of five, six years old were packed into the buses and taken away to places where they had no friends, no house nearabouts. They were taken like slabs, human slabs, packing and bringing them back, it was so inhuman. That we had to fight for years and years.

Ajit Rai

Learning to be a Housewife

My days at school were very happy days; at that time there was what was known as the scholarship. I have vague recollections that, although I was pretty good at school and usually in the top seven or eight, a warning had been given to my parents that maybe unless I really did very well I may not get a scholarship because of my father's dual nationality. At the age of twelve, in 1935, I started school at the Grange School, in the senior school. At that time the headmistress was a Miss Wilson. Thanks to Miss Wilson, we grew to have a liking for reading poetry and good books. We also learned what was in those days given the name of housewifery, one day a week, in a separate building, under a Miss Warwick. We did the basic cooking, laundry, ironing, and housekeeping generally and cleaning a room. It was a

Rothschild School.

Joseph Lancaster School.

preparation for you. There are many things which thanks to that, although I say it myself, I can do beautifully. I can iron well, still. And then of course at that age of fourteen or fifteen one had to prepare oneself for work.

Sybilla Skelton

Meet you down Ellis!

Certainly in my schooldays, the highlight of my life, in summer were the two fêtes that were held in Walpole Park. The Philanthropic Fête and the Hospital Fête. As a schoolgirl your life revolved around it

and who you were going to the fête with. It was almost like the passing out ball! It was quite a big affair in Walpole Park. All sorts of sideshows, the mile of pennies which was started off by the Mayor in his chain and then the idea was that if you could achieve the mile you got however many pennies they put to make up the mile. It ended with a firework display. We're talking about the thirties. Of course the war finished it. Certainly when you were a schoolgirl it was the place to meet your opposite numbers from the boys' school, you know. Or you met your boyfriends near the school, near the bottom of Ellis Road, which runs up the side of Lammas Park. And the girls cycled down one way and the boys cycled down the other way and you met at the end lamp-post at the end of the road. Years later, one of my neighbours looked at me and said, 'You were one of the girls who used to meet the boys under the lamp-post.' Years and years afterwards. It was 'Meet you down Ellis! Yes, meet you down Ellis!'

Viv Holding

Gymslips

I'm wearing a pleated gymslip in the photograph. It was meant to be this short. In the winter you wore a woollen jumper with it and in the summer a cream blouse. Later on we had alpaca dresses for the summer. We always wore hats, velour in the winter and Panama in the summer. Anybody who failed to wear a hat would probably find

Edna Razzelle at the Ealing County School in 1930.

Christchurch School, 1931. Dick Adams is at the back with glasses; Betty Rosier is seated in the second row, second on the right.

33

John Cameron, on the left, in 1916.

herself in trouble. There was no eating in the street! The headmistress was very strict.

Edna Razzelle

Class Six

I'm the one in the back wearing glasses. I was really self-conscious about wearing them but as I was fairly big I didn't get teased. I can remember the names of every single one of those children. Betty Rosier, everybody liked her: she was the nicest girl you ever met.

Dick Adams

Nits

I went to North Ealing School in Pitshanger Lane. I remember the school nurse coming to check our hair for nits. Class by class, we would go into a room set aside and she would plough through your hair, parting it this way and that with a fine comb. When you came out everybody would look at you, like you had leprosy. Ugh! I never had them, thank goodness but if you did you had your hair washed in vinegar.

Doreen McDermott

My Father

My father, John Cameron, went to Alexandra Road School during the First World War. He was a good footballer and played for Heston School boys. He ran for the Thames Valley Harriers and swam for Heston, winning a cup. He remembers swimming in the Thames at Isleworth and feeling the sandy bottom beneath his feet. The water then was clear and clean!

Andrea Cameron

CHAPTER 3

Working Life

Filming The Ladykillers *at Ealing Studios, 1955.*

Soapsud Island

Acton had scores of laundries, all in the south of the town. There was hardly a street that had not got three or four of them. That's why the area became known as Soapsud Island.

Tommy Harwood

Black Beetles

I started work when I was fourteen at the new Grosvenor Laundry. Left school on the Friday and went there and got the job on the Monday. My mother had always worked in the laundry and all my sisters and brothers as well. Mum was a best silk

Staff at the Thistle Laundry.

washer and my sisters were ironers. I've done everything in the laundry, even to ironing pure silk stockings and the raising of the initials on the pillow slips and sheets – for the ladies, you know. The only thing that worried me was the black beetles. You put your hand in the sheets and you got a few black beetles – cockroaches – frightened me to death! They used to come out to get in the warmth. They loved white sheets, anything white. They moved! They were just like racehorses! I used to run away from them, to tell you the truth. I shook my coat before I went home in case there was anything in the sleeves. I didn't like to tread on them. They go crack, they don't half go crack! The others used to say to me, 'What's the matter with you?' and I'd say, 'Check my coat before I get out of here, will you? I'm not putting it on yet!'

Phyllis Harold

The Hydros

Those hydros [dryers] weren't half big – cylinder things. And you had to pack 'em a certain way, all the clothing – if you didn't they wouldn't blinking run. I didn't actually see it but there was a terrible accident on the hydro. There was a shout and a scream. I think it was the man that put the belts on and he went to put this belt on without shutting down. He put his hand on the belt

The hydros at Baldwin's Empire Laundry, Acton.

The calender girls at Spring Grove Laundry, Chiswick.

to swing it round and got caught up in it. Oh, it made me go cold. Good job I didn't see it. I said, 'Why did he do it like that? Why didn't he shut it down?' It killed him. They couldn't get him off fast enough.

Bill Minter

Broken Date

You never knew: you'd be courting and all ready to meet your boyfriend when you'd hear 'Eight o'clock tonight, ladies!' I said, 'I've got a date with a boyfriend,' and she, the missis, said, 'Well you'll have to break it, won't you?' and she gave me my full title there, Evelyn, she says, 'You'll have to break it, won't you, eh Evelyn?'

Dolly Chapell

The Calender Girls

I used to work in the Kingsland Laundry. I started off packing. We used to shake out the handkerchiefs, hundreds of them. That was before we got the calender. That was a big machine that you put the sheets and the tablecloths through, like a big roller. The calender girls were very lively. Singing all the time you know, 'When I grow too old to dream', I remember.

Rose Beattie

Packing

I really did like packing. When you pack, you see the beauty of the work, when it's all finished. That's what I really liked. You stood all the time. First of all you had to

Sorting and packing, Spring Grove.

Irons and calenders at the Thistle Laundry.

make your racks – there were racks round the room and all the numbers on the racks. Then you get all the work. You start off with the bath-towels: you go all round your racks with them. Then you have your trolley-load of sheets, do them because they're big. The next part is the small work, like pillowslips and tea-towels; we called them rubbers. Then the table linen comes in, that's the tablecloths. That was all flat you see. After that you have what we call the body-linen, like vests and pants, come from upstairs. They're ironed up there. The last thing to pack would be your shirts on top. Oh, and if you've got a little hole you put your hankies in. Tuck them in, you had to line the boxes with blue tissue paper because it was nice and Mrs Simpson liked blue. You covered it

all in and then you put your laundry book on top of the blue paper. You put your box down and put the name and address on it – we used to have labels to tie on. We tied them on the box, did up the strap and then they were ready to go on the van.

Rosie Popay

Correct Way to Iron a Shirt

I was quick. I was a shirt ironer, I wasn't piece work you see. I was such a perfect folder, straight folder, sleeves all in and everything, cuffs up to the neck and everything. And of course the very, very correct way to start ironing a shirt is to iron the back of the collar. Iron the back of the collar, down the insides of the buttons, down the insides of the button holes. Then the yoke: you put your hand in and lay the yoke flat. Then you get hold of your back right in the middle where sometimes there's a pleat there. You get hold of that and you shake it so that the sleeves flow, and you've got the back. The back doesn't matter all that much because that will go out nice and smooth when you iron the top of it. Then the sleeves, the cuffs, inside the cuff first. You eliminate all the creases. That's the way it's done. Shirts have got to look like they've come out the shop.

Elizabeth Wilkinson

Ironing

I didn't do ironing. I didn't get on with gas irons. I'd never used a gas iron. I used the old flat irons, we used to spit on them to see if they were hot. The missus said, 'Can you iron?' so I said, 'Yes'. I didn't know it was a gas iron – all I could think of was there was a very nasty smell of gas, of course there was. I'd got the damn gas and not the iron alight, see. That was at the Lavender Laundry.

Dolly Chapell

First Day at Work

I can always remember my first morning at work because my dad used to come home on his bike to lunch and he was looking for me as I came straight down the road. It was a long, long road, Bollo Bridge Road. I had to run all the way because we only got an hour for lunch. My very first day – I had to run all

up the street. Oh, it was a long road and we lived right down the bottom and my Dad saw me coming. He was standing at the gate to meet me. He took hold of my hand and we both went in together. He got his cap and he polished the chair for me to sit down, my first morning at work. Then he sat me down; his first little daughter out to work.

Elizabeth Wilkinson

Royalty at the Sherborne Laundry

I'll never forgive Prince Michael of Kent getting married. I was furious about that. Because we had Prince Michael of Kent for years. Not her, we had him. Of course when they married they went into Kensington Palace and they were going to arrange the passes and we were going to go through the gates. All excited about this. And then they rang up and said well sorry, because as the Queen has Sycamore Laundry do their work, he can send his laundry with the rest of the Royal family. That used to be terribly interesting when you could see the stuff that had obviously come down through the Royal family, the coronets on it all. You know we had the Duke and Duchess of this, and Marchioness of that right down to the local postman.

Elizabeth Simpson

An Honour

We all worked in the tin shop [at the Cherry Blossom Shoe Factory in Chiswick]. Well, you know, it was an honour to work at the Cherry! You had to have your name down. One of my sisters' friends, she didn't join until she was

Filling Room girls at the Cherry Blossom Shoe Factory.

seventeen and she'd waited since she was fourteen. She'd say, "Ere, I'm going to start at the Cherry,' as if it was a marvellous job. It really was a lovely place to work.

Iris Faulkner

Make-up at the Cherry

We never wore our wedding rings. We weren't supposed to be married. You had to leave if you got married. When she was coming [Miss Milne, the supervisor], off came the lipstick, down came your cap over your eyes and off you went on your machine like this. But if she caught you with makeup you was taken to her office and she used to show you a flower and she'd say 'Can you see the lovely colours on this flower? That has no paint and powder on it, and neither do any of you girls!'

Doris Sands

Furniture Polish and Lipstick

I remember I was on fives Mansion [5lb tins of Mansion furniture polish] one day, and the weather was so hot. The polish wouldn't set and the machines had to go so slowly through the cooler because it wasn't setting. I was getting bored. So we was picking up the tins and looking at our face because they were like little mirrors, you know. Peggy had bought a new lipstick that weekend. So we was all trying on this lipstick, wasn't we, and I was saying to Peggy, 'Don't it suit me Peggy?' 'cos she's the other side of the machine, laying out, and I'm laying out this side. 'Does it suit me Peggy? Answer me, Peggy,' and she wouldn't answer. And I thought to myself, why won't she answer me. Who's standing behind me but Miss Milne! So she just got hold of my ear, made me give Peggy the lipstick back and she took me straight down to the washplace and made me wash my face. So I was caught red-handed you know!

Joan Field

Green Drawers

We had our own social club, opera and dramatic classes. Miss Wiggington, our Wiggy, was the dancing teacher. We used to put this yearly concert on. We had to wear very frilly frocks with plenty of bows all over but your knickers had to come just below your knees and even when you were doing your gym you had a lovely Grecian little slip on but you still had these long green drawers on underneath. They were the bane of our life, those green drawers.

Doris Sands

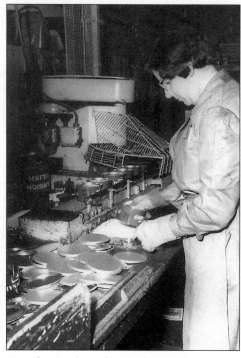

Dorothy Croft in the tin shop at the Cherry, 1960s. Notice the 'mirror' lids.

Long green drawers for the Cherry girls.

Stan Whetlor, aged fifteen, and Mr Hudson, 1935.

The Blower

When the blower went at eight minutes to two, I got on my bike, on the road and in the factory in eight minutes. That eight minutes in Chiswick everyone knew. As soon as that went twice; eight minutes. Quick, everybody ran. Eight minutes to eight and eight minutes to two. Run like mad, round the corner, round by the Feathers, weren't we. In one blue surge because we wore navy blue before the war and green after the war. It was one blue surge right round the corner and over to the club, through William Street.

Doris Sands

The Chosen Few

Most of the girls that had a journey dressed up to come to work. They came down in floods of girls, they were really and truly smart, with gloves on, handbags and shoes, everything to match just to go to work in the Cherry, and if you didn't know, you'd say they all worked in the office they were turned out that well, but they didn't. We were lucky to work in the Cherry, we were the chosen few to go there.

Joan Field

Boot Polish

I went to work at the Cherry Blossom. I left Hogarth School at fourteen in 1934 and was one of the elite van boys as they used to call us. I worked on Mr Hudson's van. When it rained it was a nightmare to most of the van boys at the Cherry Blossom. We used to have to go down to the garage every day we come in, and we used to hose it all down, sponge it, leather it and when it was dry we used to have to do the tyres, with Cherry Blossom boot polish on the outside, the back wheels and the spare wheels that was underneath the lorry at the back, wash down the sides, blackened with boot polish. The front wheels we used to have to jack up and do the inside and the outside. So when we went to work the next morning the van looked lovely.

Stan Whetlor

Scott of the Antarctic

Most of the close-up shots were filmed in the biggest stage with wind machines

Stan in the RNVR, 1940. All the girls at the Cherry fancied him.

blowing and a lot of ground up plastic dropped down so there was a constant white mist. Because in the Arctic you get white out. Of course you couldn't film the real thing. In fact the reason I got such terrible catarrh was due to spending days and weeks in there. In the end we were all issued with masks, because you couldn't breathe in the stuff.

Roy Gough

Stank like Hell

We had to send a crew down to Antarctica, not merely to get authentic icebergs, but the Emperor penguins. There's nowhere else you can find them. Back at Ealing we had the main big studio. We had a big cyclorama and we had a problem about the right material for the snow. In the end we had a chemical expert who experimented and the first effective white snow he produced was made from drainage products. It was brilliant white, but it stank like hell – urea – so he had to go back to the drawing board or the test tube or whatever. And he finally produced some very good snow.

Anon.

Continuity at Ealing Studios

Bloomin' hard work! A lot easier now of course then because they take polaroids. When I first started you had to do everything on your notes, you had to keep a diary and record every moment of every day. You had to type a continuity sheet for every shot with all the takes and the prints, type out all the dialogue and the action. And of course in those days it was

Filming Scott of the Antarctic, *Ealing Studios, 1948.*

typing with carbons, none of this photocopying. You had to make notes of what everyone was wearing and which direction they came in and out. You would say 'Excuse me you had your scarf...' and they would say, 'Oh no I didn't,' and you couldn't argue with a star if they wanted it that way. Meanwhile you made a note: 'Miss so and so insisted, insisted, her scarf went that way' to cover yourself. Words might be said very loudly in rushes. You might be sitting during rushes, thinking 'Oh my God!' The editor would say 'Where was the continuity girl? Was she awake?'

Paddy Porter

Down on his Uppers

At the time they were making *Scott* I was still a very new photographer and assisting my boss, who was a bit of a snob, in the still studio and he called me down one day and he said 'Gough'. He was the only man on the film unit who called me by my surname. He said 'As you know I only photograph the really big names. There's a young man, seems a nice enough young man, who wants his photograph taken, but he's not important enough for me, so perhaps you'd go into the studio and take a few shots.' So I went in to the studio and this young man got up and said 'Hello, I'm Kenny [Kenneth] More,' and I said, 'I'm Roy,' and that was the very first film job he had. He was down on his uppers. I took that picture of him, and he used it for the front page of his autobiography. Very nice chap.

Roy Gough

Money for Old Rope

Ladykillers was huge fun; it was huge fun partly because Katie Johnson was such an absolutely enchanting little old lady. She was exactly by nature as she was in the film. I don't know where she lived but we decided because she was elderly, she was going to be put up. In those days in Ealing, you didn't put people up in grand hotels. We found her a boarding house on Ealing Common and I said, 'We'll pick you up every morning at 8.30,' and she said, 'Oh, I can walk to the studios, it's not very far.' And I said, 'No, Katie, we'll pick you up.' And certainly, in those days, you called actors for the time you think you're going to need them and it always turns out to be an hour and a half before you do need them. And I had called Alec and we had not used him for four hours or something, he'd been sitting in the dressing room getting crosser and crosser. And so he came on extremely cross and so did Katie, who had also been waiting. I thought I could rely on Katie and said, 'Terribly sorry, Katie: you've been here for

Peter Sellers, Herbert Lom, Alec Guinness and Alexander Mackendrick on the set of The Ladykillers *in 1955.*

Filming The Maggie *at Crinan, Scotland, 1954.*

four hours and we haven't used you, I must apologize.' 'Oh,' she said, 'that's perfectly all right. After all, I'm paid, aren't I? It's money for old rope.' And of course, poor Alec was totally unable to throw his little number after that.

Tom Pevsner

Diana Dors

One day they said, 'We've got a young actress coming in the studio and I want you to take some photographs of her.' So I got the camera set up in the studio and waited and in bounced this plump young woman –

she must have been about seventeen then – and plonked herself down and fell right out of her dress! And I was so embarrassed, tripping over the lights, and she said, 'Whoops!' and put herself back again. Diana Dors was to Ealing a breath of fresh air.

Roy Gough

Puffer Disaster

There's a scene on the *Maggie*, the puffers film. Paul Douglas, the American, is waiting for the puffer to pick him up from some deserted jetty somewhere. The puffer, which is run by two drunken Scotsmen and a boy,

47

is supposed to pick him up but they mistakenly plough straight through the jetty leaving him on the end, cut off from the land with a flock of Highland cattle. And so we had to build the jetty and the section that had to be broken we built out of balsa wood so it would collapse easily, because it was a one-off thing. Big, big occasion, three cameras which was very rare at that time, everybody ready, Paul Douglas on the end of this thing... and we thought we'd better have a rehearsal. Puffers are actually ridiculous flat bottom boats, they've got very weak engines and they're very approximate pieces of equipment. Anyway, we had a rehearsal and the puffer approached the jetty and Sandy [Mackendrick] said, 'Yes,

that's fine. OK, now stop and we'll go for a take'. And I said 'Stop' and everybody else said 'Stop' and the puffer just went on and ploughed straight through the jetty which had taken months to build and the cameras weren't turning. So everybody kind of went very, very quiet.

Tom Pevsner

Re-touching

I was only a second class re-toucher so I used to re-touch occasionally. You'd work on the negatives and you would use a knife, you'd put re-touching medium over the surface,

Alec Guinness and Stanley Holloway in The Lavender Hill Mob, *filmed partly in Gunnersbury Park in 1951.*

some kind of sticky substance, like a black paint with ox-gruel in it. Then you'd scrape away with the knife anything that was dark, like a pimple. And the bags under the eyes you'd scrape that away, and if there was a white mark you used to have to fill them in with a pencil to smooth the skin. The actual size of the negative was ten inches by eight inches, so it was pin sharp and the complexions actually didn't look all that wonderful. It was quite time-consuming, but then you see hundreds of photographs would be printed from those negatives so it was worth doing. If they didn't have enough eyelashes you'd do the eyelashes in with a knife. You always wanted your star to look wonderful.

Joan McQueen

Robin at the Gate

Robin at the Gate was quite a simple man in a way, and all the actors and actresses used to come in and say 'Hello Robin' and he'd pass them through the gate. They'd call him Robin and he'd call them Mr So-and-so and this was his whole life. When the studio closed, his life finished and he died within a few months.

Roy Gough

The End of it All

We were shooting and suddenly Hal Mason came round and said, 'Stop shooting boys, I have an announcement to make. I regret to have to tell you...' – Sir Michael [Balcon] didn't come on the set, I don't think he could face it – 'that I have to say that the studios have ceased production.' Why did they do it at about half past three in the afternoon without giving us any notice at all? But the reason is it was all in the evening papers – we wouldn't have known until we'd read them. And a lot of people still feel very bitter about that. It was like the end of the world.

Roy Gough

Motorbike Messenger

Everyone knew, when they were coming up to sixteen, the possibility of going on the motorcycles – going on the motor as it was called. There was money in it, there was kudos. Oh I mean, 'He's on the motors' – it's a big thing, you know. We weren't allowed to go around with another messenger; they done it because it was breaking the rules. And that was called wozzalling in most places. In Ealing messengers were known as mergers and the telegrams were mergs. Tubby Appleby was in the Home Guard. He got the Home Guard motor cycle, which was a 350 BSA. And I said, 'Let's have a ride on it.' I went down the Ealing Road and he said don't touch this and don't touch that. By the way, all the controls were different in those days. You could control the air and the petrol, it wasn't just about pressing your foot on the pedal, and you could advance and retard the ignition. I'd already got the ignition retarded, and I swung round St Mary's and just on the bit of the South Ealing Road, I pushed the ignition forward and vhmmm, shot forward. I was doing eighty at the bottom of the road. I'd never been so fast in my life, and eighty on a motorcycle closes your nose you know, you can't breathe.

Jim Janus

Jim Burch in the front, Jim Janus on the ground, with Tubby Appleby behind.

Jim Burch, messenger boy.

The Milk Round

They were in France, Fred and Wally, after the First World War. My brother Wally, he was gassed wasn't he, with the mustard gas, and Fred, he had a bullet through his face. And it went right through him and killed his mate at the side of him. After the war they couldn't go back to their trade because they were so young; when they went to the war they didn't finish their apprenticeship. You see one was going to be an electrician and one was going to be a stonemason but they never finished their time, and when they were out of work after the war they took any job. Fred worked for the dairies and he got my youngest brother Charlie in there. Charlie, was on the milk round with the barrow. I remember they used to go into the public house after they'd done their rounds, and they used to take bets for their friends in the public house. When Charlie was late and didn't get up my mum used to send me

Charlie Brewer with his milk float in the 1920s.

out instead of him. And I hated it, because it was ever so dark. They used to do two rounds, you see, sometimes three rounds a day. Like one before breakfast, then the one after and then there was one in the afternoon. I used to get scared stiff in the mornings, it was so dark. But nothing happened to us. When you think of it there was no hygiene, no bottles. We used to dip these things in the urns.

Violet Brewer

Toothpaste Tubes

I left school at fourteen and went to work at Macleans. I earned 13s a week. I started screwing the tops on the tubes. You had the screw top lid at the bottom, with an open case

made of a leaded-like material. One girl would take one of these tubes and put it up to the machine to fill it with toothpaste. That would go round and the machine would automatically squash the end down. Then they'd fall off one by one onto the belt, and the same procedure went on there. You had three people screwing the tops to make certain they were tight, and these used to make your fingers raw, 'cos they were in an eight-sided shape, they were. So we had our fingers covered with plaster to save them getting too sore.

Mary Huxley

Call Boy

I started as a walk-on at the Chiswick Empire, doing pageboys, things like that.

51

Then I got the job of call boy. I was doing a day job at the factory and in the evenings I was at the theatre. The call boy stands near the stage and the Stage Manager calls him to go up into the dressing room area to call people when they had to stand by to go on stage. There was no PA system in those days, and complete silence in the dressing rooms, and they didn't know what was going on the stage so I used to go up and prompt them.

Sybil Thorndyke came round with a play called *The Distaff Side*. She was a very nice lady. On Saturday nights it was our practice to be quite nice and pleasant towards the cast, because they were going on to the next date, and we used to wish them well you know, because we might get a tip. Our wages were 10s a week. And so we used to say goodnight and Sybil Thorndyke was very generous. I got 3s 6d, which was an outstanding amount in those days, because usually it was just a shilling or sixpence. On another occasion we had Harry Lauder, he was a very old Scottish comedian, well known for his meanness. The stage-door keeper said to me, 'The last time Harry Lauder was here he gave me a photograph of himself and that was the tip'. So anyway we waited and Mr Harry Lauder came up and he walked straight past me and went up to the stage door man and said 'I mind the last time I was here, did I not give you a photo of myself?' and the stage-door keeper said 'Yes, you did.' So he said, 'Well, you give it to me and I'll sign it.' That was his tip!

Earl Kay

Corsets and Brazil Nuts

I started at Mrs Perrin's haberdashery shop in Brentford High Street. She made these corsets for older women with big busts and big hips. I used to have to measure them. I used to throw the tape round and catch it the other side. It was long hours: I started at eight and I didn't finish till seven most days of the week, eight on Fridays and nine on Saturdays, which meant I couldn't go dancing on a Saturday. I got fed up with the long hours so on my half day I went over to Greenford and got a job at Lyons. I was in the nut room and most of that was shelling brazils. They were partly cracked and we all used to sit round a table and dig our knife in and hook them out. Then we had three sieves, one was for whole ones, and one was for cracked ones and one was for bad ones. We used to sing a lot. We used to come home with a song sheet and sing all the way home from West Ealing because we couldn't afford the fare; we had to walk back to Brentford.

Katherine Cowper

Early Wooden Aircraft

I got this job at General Aircraft, at Hanworth Air Park. They built the BA Swallow which was used as a trainer in the early part of the war. I remember one crashing in Feltham High Street early one morning like a big pile of firewood. All these aeroplanes were built mainly of wood and fabric. It took off on its own, the bloke was warming it up and it jumped the chocks, took off on its own over the houses and dived in the yard at the back of the houses. They built a little thing called a Cygnet, which was a side-by-side two-seater. Pretty little aeroplane, it came to nothing because the war came along, but you could drive it round the track almost like a car. Then we got on to Spitfire wings, tailplanes and wing tips for the Spitfire.

Beer swilling at Fuller, Smith and Turner, 1960s.

I got a job at Fairey Aviation in Hayes, in the fuselage shop. The head of the company, Sir Richard Fairey, was still alive in those days and they built the Swordfish, the famous Swordfish. Fairey's built all naval aircraft and they were all completely different to anybody else's idea of building aeroplanes. The fuselage was always built in the same way a boat is built, upside down and then turned over and finished off. They used to turn the fuselage over and fill it up full of water to see if it leaked. Before the war there was a big bout of whooping cough and they'd take the kids up in a Monospar about 8,000ft, which was supposed to be a cure for whooping cough. Of course they weren't pressurized aircraft so they were all puffing a bit at 8,000ft.

Tony Lackerstein

Copper Boy at Fuller's Brewery

The best job I had was when I was copper boy. I used to sit and watch the beer boil. When the beer came up you had to shout, 'Coming up!' and they'd open the dampers till it got its momentum. The Head Brewer said to me ' Tim, if you let that beer boil over the wall you'll be here tonight white-washing it again and you won't get paid.' So you made sure you didn't! When I approached twenty-one they said to me, 'We're moving you down now into the cementing room and you will get a man's pay now.' So I said, 'Thanks very much, how much is that then?' 'About 30s a week.' I worked down there and they said, 'Do you want to go on the overtime list?' so I said 'Yes please, anything to earn more money,' so you did four hours work for 1s 6d per hour. That was 6s, a lot of money then. The work was hard, forty-five hours a week and Saturdays as well. The job consisted of cleaning the copper squares where the beer had been in fermenting. You had to get in and squeeze the yeast out that was left. That went through a press and the best yeast went to Marmite and the other went into cattle food. Then you got in and you had a pumice stone crushed up and a broom, and scrubbed all around the squares.

Tim Gale

In Service

I worked for a family in Corfton Road; it's up from Ealing Broadway station. You had everything to do. You had to be up and have the gentleman's bath run by seven o'clock in the morning and the stove in the kitchen had to be filled at night to make sure that the water was very hot next day. I was fourteen when I first went. There was two of us went because it was a fairly big house, but after a while the other girl left and I was on my own. You started work at seven and you were lucky if you were in bed by midnight. Some nights I fell asleep with me uniform on. We used to wear uniform – the morning uniform and the afternoon uniform. You lived for your half day: sometimes it didn't start till three o'clock and you had to be in by ten o'clock at night. And when you got home there used to be all these dirty dishes waiting for you to start on. They didn't treat their maids like they should have done.

Elizabeth Yates

Window Cleaning

My father was a window cleaner. He learned all about horses in the Army in the First World War, but there were fewer about the time I was born (1922). He worked for T&S Window Cleaning Company. He was the foreman and did everything, got the work, took the money, paid the men, put the rest in the bank. Then he thought, 'I'm stupid doing all this,' and soon he started up on his own. He was reasonably successful until old Hitler started smashing all the windows. He used to do all the big windows down the High Street and the Broadway and round by the station and Haven Green. He earned about three quid a week, which was reasonable, except when it rained of course – then nobody wanted their windows cleaned.

Dick Adams

Cleaning windows in Ealing, 1930s.

Dick Adams' father.

Woolf's Rubber Factory

Horrible! Not what any human being can stand. All over dirt, no rules, no unions, no facilities, no rights to the workers. It was the rule of the jungle. The foremen, they were shouting at our people – 'Oi, you!' – they were so rude. It was indecent behaviour that no decent person can stand. Our people had to stand that type of treatment simply because they were fearing that if they would object or retaliate they might be chucked out, dismissed and they couldn't find a job anywhere. That was the fear in their minds which was stopping them reacting to that treatment.

Ajit Rai

Gunnersbury Stables

In 1935 Dad was offered a job in Gunnersbury Park as horse-keeper. There were several cylinder mowers, which the horses pulled, cutting all the fields. He was the one that was responsible for the horses, especially at night. Dad was the one who had to look after them if they were ill. We'd tell him the horses were bad, and he'd go down there at about two in the morning and that would be the last you'd see of him until breakfast time. He used to say a horse was lovely, you could even sleep with it. He was a very dedicated man to his horses. The bathroom was stacked out with all the horse oils and liniments. If you hurt yourself he'd say, 'You want a bit of horse oil on you.'

Betty Winnett

Bernard Collis on his tractor, 1945.

Working for the Rothschilds

I started work in 1919 when I was fourteen. My grandmother lived in Antrobus Road where the head gardener of the Rothschilds lived and my grandma was saying to him that I was leaving school and got to find a job somewhere, so he asked if I could have an interview up there. He walked me all the way to Gunnersbury Park and I had an interview with Mr Reynolds, the bailiff. My first jobs were to clean the boots and shoes belonging to the head gardener and the family, all the sons and daughters. After that I used to clean the knives, after that I used to chop the wood and take the logs, the coal, all in their bins, into the kitchen and be ready for the next day. I used to go down and collect the milk from the dairy. They had their own herd of cattle, you know. I used to scrub all the stonework, clean the

Charles Smith on his cylinder mower at Gunnersbury Park, 1935.

Mike Clarke (on the left), one of Robert's four brothers at Brentford Market.

windows, clean the chickens out, collect the eggs. I got paid 10s a week.

Bernard Collis

Portering at Brentford Market

I was a market porter. I used to deliver the fruit and vegetables to the greengrocers' wagons when they bought them from the stands at Brentford Market. I had four brothers in there as well. It was all family, local people from Brentford, Chiswick, Greenford. When I was there the Clarkes and the Welsleys were the two biggest families. There were seven Welsleys and

five Clarkes working in there, brothers from well known local families.. Everyone knew everyone else.

The market was opened six days a week. We used to start at four, especially in the summer when the strawberry season and the soft fruit was in; we started earlier sometimes, at two o'clock, when you had unloading to do. Strawberry season you earned money, you used to have four or five thousand trays of strawberries in a night – that's why you used to come in at two o'clock. Usually you'd be on the job at five; that would give you an hour to get the show out and then the market opened officially at six o'clock for delivery. Of course with your wages, you was only paid by what you moved. If you didn't do no work you didn't get paid. When you unloaded from the delivery wagon you were paid 1s 9d a ton; everything was in tonnage. Then when you took the vegetables from the stall to the greengrocers they paid a portage, that was a penny on a box of apples, halfpenny on a box of mushrooms, threepence on a bag of potatoes, that was your portage. When you got a slip, your portage was added underneath. The firm charged you for doing that, and although they paid you a retaining fee, they charged you sixpence in the pound to do the books up, to give you the wages at the end of the week. But that entitled you to look at the books at any time. You could work with who you

wanted to: if anyone was short of a porter you could go and pick up his stuff and deliver it. You collected portage, you hung on to the ticket and then you showed it at the end of the day and that money was then passed to you. The money was seasonal. You could always go to other stalls to see if they needed work. They had a coffee shop in there and if you ever landed out of work you could always go in there and clean the tables.

If it was a rich greengrocer they had someone that permanently stayed on the wagon and we unloaded it, stacked it and he stayed with the wagon to stop pilfering. A lot of the porters started to open little shops with any extra stuff they could get away with, but you just reported it and if

Porters at Brentford Market: Reg Routledge and Bill Fowler.

Brentford Docks.

you were clever you was able to pilfer somebody else's to make your losses up. People used to bring in stolen goods; you could buy anything you wanted. The police wandered round every so often and one or two would get caught. Even cars, they'd take your car and replace it with the same model but a newer year with your registration on it. Anything you could buy – you only had to put the word in the market and it appeared. Hell of a lot of pilfering from the stands: a lot of porters were caught and lost their jobs, they tried to clamp down on it.

With the old Brentford market it was that small, the greengrocer could walk all the way round because the stands were so near. The women greengrocers treated you worse than the men. They swore at you and they knew their trade. They swore at you and you swore back at them, if you was that way inclined. There were

certain times when you'd got to swear, you've got to come down to their level otherwise they just took the mickey out of you, and made your life worse. You used to take your own children in and they used to help. We used to take them on the backs of the tracks for a ride, they enjoyed it. They did a sponsored race from Kew Bridge to the Star and Garter Hotel, a relay race pulling a barrow-load of fruit and veg, apples and oranges. All the fruit that was pulled there used to go into the home for disabled soldiers and sailors. You used to get a lot of nuns come in collecting, going round asking if there was any unwanted vegetables or fruit, for the orphanages. Then you got the zoos coming for the wild animals and they used to take all the rotten fruit that couldn't be sold.

Robert Clarke

59

Loading the barges

We used to serve all Hayes and Southall with cargo and we used to take the sleepers, shiploads of sleepers for the Great Western Railway to lay on the tracks. We used to take sugar and oranges to Keeley and Toms which was a jam factory in Southall, sugar, cocoa beans and nuts to Nestlé's milk factory at Hayes, timber to HMV, they used to make the gramophones and pianos and all that sort of thing. Timber to Uxbridge and Watford, wood pulp up to Croxley. Safety regulations came into it a lot. We used to have inspectors come down; trade unions had rules regarding lifting and all that sort of thing. You was only allowed to lift what you could lift, say there was two of us, we'd pick up a sack of wheat, say two hundredweight. You couldn't pick it up on your own. I've seen women on boats get hold of hundredweight boxes of sugar and tea and load them on their backs. One woman, a big woman she was, she used to say to her husband, 'Come on let me have a go at that' and she'd push him out of the way and she'd get this bag of sugar and load it on the boat, she'd step down and just plant it. They could do it as good as men, 'cos they had to work as hard as men, those women on the boats, had to work very hard, all hours, all night.

Tom Bowles

The Good Old Days?

I got a job at Kew Bridge Pumping Station. The shifts were two till ten, ten till six, six to two. This was round the clock. People fitted into that time. It meant that some would be paid overtime for their Sunday work and Christmas Day. And that again was something which could have led to a few niggles until they were sorted out by Mr Joyce and Mr Wailes. Because if they were working over Christmas time they would get more money and this was always carefully recorded so that next Bank Holiday, someone else would get a crack of the whip. As a young man I got the wrong idea when I heard them arguing about weekend and Christmas, because I thought how awful it was to work over Christmas. Then I realized they were struggling in order to work over Christmas time because there was money in it. That was one of my first lessons. Those chaps worked their bloody guts out, day in day out, and they worked very hard, scraping the boilers, shovelling the coal. If you went into that stoke hole, the workshop there, you'd find a lot of smelly men sweating their guts out on hard work. We mustn't look back on 'the good old days' because they weren't all that good.

Tony Oldfield

Not All Doom and Gloom

I left school to become an office boy at General Aircraft, but it was thought that working in the machine shops would be more educational. I was earning the princely sum of 8s 6d a week, but my brother Ernest got me a job at the Sperry Gyroscope Company on the Great West Road where he was then working, for 13s 9d a week. Cycling each day from Feltham to Brentford and back certainly kept me fit. When the war broke out in 1939, the work at Sperry's was considered to be so important to the war effort that all the staff were declared to be in 'reserved occupations'. We were making

Kew Bridge Pumping Station, 1957.

instruments for aircraft and warships and other top-secret projects. All the Great West Road factories were working day and night, during those dark and dangerous days. However, all was not doom and gloom. We started a works concert party under the watchful eye of Harry Thomas, a former music hall singer and performer, and soon we were not only entertaining our fellow workmates, but giving charity and troop shows. One evening we were booked to give a show at the Gunnersbury Gunsight, set in part of the park. I was met at the bus stop by the organizer on a very dark night, and he was to escort us past the sentry. As we proceeded down the little lane a very loud voice shouted 'Halt! who goes there?' My legs turned to jelly, and I don't think I could have spoken if I had wanted to, to some being who no doubt was pointing a rifle with bayonet at me in the dark, but I could not see. My escort told the sentry I was one of the 'entertainers' and we were allowed to pass.

Eddie Menday

Hard Work and Dirty Work

I worked in HMV, His Master's Voice, in Hayes. Finished up a French polisher, polishing cabinets, televisions. Then for thirty-one years I worked in a concrete firm, down in South West Road, Girling's Stone. We were making air-raid shelters and working out in the open, winter and summer. My sister and I, we had moulds, wooden moulds, and we used to have to grease them – we had a bucket of grease – grease 'em down and then put all the sides together, and then the men would fill them up with concrete and then vibrate them with the vibrator so they were set. When they were set they would dismantle the concrete mould and turn them out. Outside, winter and summer, for thirty-one years. There was a big gang of us. We had so much to do in one day, and if you went over the top of what you had to do, then you had what they called bonus. If you come home from there with about £4 or £5, you was well off. I did that winter and summer in the open, when it rained, when it snowed. We started making floor and roof beams. We used to have to grease all that; we used to put brushes on a long stick like a broom handle and we used to have a bucket and dip it in there, my sister and I, and we used to have to grease it all. Then we had like wooden shutters but they were in the shape of ridges and we used to have to grease both sides of them and then we put them all together. There were about sixteen or eighteen beams, we used to have to grease the cores – they were all steel. Then they put the beams in the concrete and they used to slide these beams into the steel cores. Then they put the rest over the top and covered them with concrete. When they were set in the afternoon they used to have a big instrument to pull all the cores right out. We used to have to do that every day. It was hard work and it was dirty work, we got elevenpence an hour for that.

Cissy Randall

Keeping Up with the Hairdos

Well in those days, the 1950s, it was the Perry Como, the Cliff Richard, the Rock Hudson and all that. One of the hairstyles was like this, all the Kray twins used to have that sort of hairstyle didn't they, all the

David Read in Acton Lane, 1999. Old petrol pumps are one of the many things he collects.

Roger Sullivan Adams, 1954.

barbers' shops closing down. At Coles at Chiswick Park station, there used to be six men there, and it went down to two, or one and a half to be exact – a part-timer. We had four in our shop; just the governor and me ended up in there. You just struggled, had to go and find work outside, on your day off go to the hospital and cut hair there, things like that. But we survived. We kidded we could do the long hair and we got away with it, the customer didn't know anything about it, just thin it out and so on.

Roger Sullivan-Adams

Mellow Yellow

I was very keen on music and I became a DJ. That was back in 1969. I was one of the first mobile DJs. I did that for twenty-odd years. I used to do the Horse of the Year Show at Earl's Court; I used to work virtually every weekend. I called myself 'mellow yellow'. I made all my own equipment and travelled round in a Transit van. I played the Beatles, of course, and the Rolling Stones. Then it was Heavy Metal, Led Zeppelin, Black Sabbath. I've got hundreds of records. To keep up with the charts I bought six or eight records a week. Every Friday I used to go to 'Spinning Disc' in Chiswick and buy Chart Climbers.

David Read

tearaways. The teddy boys went for the DA or District Attorney, commonly known as – excuse me – the duck's arse. They used to all have hair nets, you'd get these big sort of lorry drivers sitting there with hair nets on their heads, underneath the hair dryers. In the sixties, Mick Jagger and the Rolling Stones, they closed thousands of barber shops, didn't they – completely ruined the trade. It was the survival of the fittest. Me and my governor stuck it out and pretended we could handle the long hair, because all the barbers didn't know how to cut the long hair. Suddenly all these people grew their hair but didn't need a haircut for two years. It grows half an inch a month, hair, so you got six inches or even twelve inches of hair down their back. Just think, all these

CHAPTER 4
Hard Times

Rattenburys, in Brentford High Street, sold new goods at no. 288 and had a pawnbroking business at 289. It closed in 1968.

Diddle'em Clubs

They had what they called diddle'em clubs, and they did diddle them as well. You paid a farthing the first week, a ha'penny the next week, a penny the next week and then twopence, fourpence and eightpence. It doubled itself each week you see gradually, as time got on, people couldn't manage to pay that double amount, so they lost what they had paid 'cos they had to pay right to the end of the amount that was set you see. That was how it came to be called the diddle'em club. Every Monday morning Boshers used to be full up with people pawning their suits.

Rosie Popay

Slogging Life

My mum had thirteen of us, see, and she died at forty-five. She was a lovely mum. Worn out, poor thing, 'cos we got lower and lower. She used to go out ironing till ten, twelve at night. What a slogging life it was in them days. No machines like they got now. Money was scarce; a ha'penny weren't worth nothing.

Lilian Sneaden

The Pawnshop

When I was about ten, I used to take my father's blue serge suit, the only one he had, down to Rattenbury's or Foster's pawnshop in Brentford. It went in on the Monday, pawned for 2s 6d, and redeemed on the Friday for him to wear playing dominoes for pints at the North Star pub. He never knew that mother pawned it. She was often broke by Wednesday but Friday was pay day so we could always get the suit back. Sometimes she made up a parcel with things like a pillowcase, a tablecloth, a sheet and a towel which could all be pawned during the week for about 1s 3d. I was embarrassed walking down the street with the parcel because everybody knew what that meant. Occasionally we pawned his fob watch.

Vera Burrows

Tallyman

I lived down in Bollo Bridge Road when Mother was only in these two rooms. I remember that she could never afford to go out and buy me anything in the shops – a coat or anything. I can really remember standing in the dark passage with my face against the street door, crying because I hadn't got a coat. My mother took me to a shop in Hammersmith, a big clothiers, they serviced all the poor. They were well known for being the tallymen. She took me and I chose this coat and she paid a shilling a week for it. The tallyman would call once a week.

Elizabeth Wilkinson

The Tallymen and the Co-op

A lot of people used the tallymen. They used to come round with a case of things and persuade people to buy them and then they were in debt to this firm and often the things were very inferior; the tallymen charged more than the value of the article. I can remember the tallyman used to come to the family next door and when they moved he said to my mother would she like to, and she said. 'No, I would not! I shop at the Co-op!'

Doris Ashby

Cruelty

I was always very poor. My mother worked at a laundry, like everybody else. She spent her whole life there. I had four brothers, and each and every one of us were taught that the moment you could walk you started working. It was as bad as that. Acton Baths was a godsend. I used to go up there every Saturday and take my own soap, the whole family had to do it. After I was about eleven my stepfather came in. Bad time, really

One of the slipper baths at Brentford public baths.

cruel: he wanted to get rid of me because I was another mouth, he didn't want to feed me, he said so. I left home at twelve, couldn't take no more beatings. I had no life really, I was under threat all the time.

George Joel

Drowning

I was nine years of age when me mum drowned. Me dad used to suffer bad with ulcers, from the First World War and the gassing and that, and he took ill when we were out at the Surrey Commercial Dock on the Thames to load timber, and got taken to the Royal Free Hospital. Me uncle came down from Brentford to see the barge loaded and the next day decided to take it up to the Ballot Box at Horsenden Hill so as to get rid of the timber. He and me mum brought the barge back down to Brentford with the horse, like. One winter morning they started away from Brentford, got up through the first lock all right, the 'Clever Hands Lock', as we call it. It was a very frosty, snowy morning, been freezing through the night, me mum was steering the barge, she pushed the tiller over and her feet went from under her and she went into the canal, into very deep mud. All that you could see of her was her legs and her slippers sticking up in the air like. Me uncle couldn't get near the barge from the towpath because there was too much mud on either side of the canal

The Docks at Brentford on the Grand Union Canal in the 1930s.

A narrowboat between Hanwell and Brentford.

A thin, hard-worked barge horse standing on the towpath in the 1930s.

and no one could get to me mum till the police came and pulled her out. She died from suffocation in the mud. When me dad came out of hospital he said he couldn't manage all me brothers and sisters and they all ended up in Dr Barnardo's homes. There was only three of us what didn't go into care.

Tommy Osborne

Out of India

I was married in 1945 to RAF Corporal Fred Buckland. We had one child, Corinne, who was born in Kharagpur. When we came to Ealing in January 1948 I couldn't believe the intense cold weather, and the rationing – one egg each per week! I used my whole weekly ration in one day.

At first I couldn't light a fire because I didn't know you had to clean out the ashes, there were no coal fires in homes in India. Fred's mother and aunt taught me many things about life here. In India we had servants to do the cooking and housework and the dhobie took the laundry away and brought it back completed.

Rita Buckland

Buckle End of the Belt

You were trying your hardest with some of them, like the one I used to call 'Uncle'. He would think nothin', like if you hadn't done the job properly, he wouldn't think nothing about picking a piece of boat rope up and just hitting you round the ribs with it or getting his belt off, pull your trousers down and give you the buckle end of the belt.

Tommy Osborne

Off the Windrush

I am Jamaican, born and bred. We heard that England was opening up to take immigrants to help build up the country. It was after the war and everything was in a mess. My husband came over on the *Windrush*. It cost £28. I came over in December 1949. I didn't bring my children over, we gradually sent for them. It was cold and raining. The first thing I did was to buy shoes to keep my feet warm. We tried to find a place to live in, we looked for the whole day. We would knock and they would say it had gone or the sign would say 'no blacks'.

Mrs Mitchell

Grey and Boring

When I first came to this country I was shocked at the difference, the weather, grey buildings, grey sky and dull clothes. I remember having to wear a coat and sandal-like shoes. In Jamaica we wore bright comfortable clothes. I had to adapt to boring clothes and a boring environment.

Azalee Jennings

Teddy Boy Gangs

There was quite a lot of racism at Featherstone High School in Southall. We got beaten up a lot. We used to see these teddy boys, the early skinheads, their hair sharp like Elvis Presley and their trousers very tight and the shoes very sharp. They walked in a group, like ten or fifteen. They beat anybody – basically they were an aggressive type of people. Not only to people that were not their colour; they'd do it to anybody.

Rasham Samra

Moving into Southall

They were not even liking us to be their neighbours. It was not so much that we were not hardworking, that we couldn't communicate with them. It was a clash of cultures, they didn't like our food, they didn't like our dress, they didn't like it when we used to talk in our own language so that was the basis of their resentment. They couldn't tolerate our culture.

Ajit Rai

On the Dole

There wasn't much work about then. I got in a queue at the factory gates to ask for work, at Robsons of York Road. I signed up with them for a job as a labourer. I was painting chassis underneath the lorries. We used to look in the racks to see if our cards were still there, to see of any of us had been put off. Some of us were put off and then taken back on the next day when more chassis came in and more bodies were being built. We were paid by the hour. If they didn't want you any more you had your cards that day and that's it. Then you had to sign on at the Labour Exchange every day and report over the counter and you had to tell

John Rogers aged three and a half with his mother in Chiswick High Road, 1939.

John Rogers aged eighteen months with his father on Acton Green, 1937.

them there was no work. You wouldn't get paid if you were working odd jobs in between. I did do one job in between. I did a moving job for a Welsh couple who lived underneath my flat where I was living. When I got back I reported to the Labour Exchange and told them I'd been working and got ten bob for doing the job, that's all I got; they stopped my dole money, they stopped me two days' money. The dole was 21s a week. Times were very hard; by the time you'd paid your debts and your food, you didn't have much left. That was about 1931.

Fred Gibbs

Extremely Unhealthy!

We were a very poor family. My father, I'm afraid, tended to drink a lot. He was a chain smoker, he was a carpenter when he could get a job but he had a bad temper and he often lost his job, he was often unemployed. My mother never knew how much he earned. He didn't even let on when he was out of work, he kept it to himself, and he would go out at the same time and come back at the same time. He was the head of the family, you didn't question him. He was violent but he never hit me or my mother, he took it out on the furniture, the door, the dinner. If he didn't like it he threw it out. When he was sober he was a very nice man, gentle, very old – he was born in 1883 and was fifty-two when I was born. He played professional football for Fulham before the First World War. He was ruined in the trenches, his nerves were shattered and that's when he took to alcohol and smoking. My mother was never very well, she had TB, and she couldn't go out to work so there was never much money coming in. We lived in a rented top-floor flat, in a house in Acton. That was on the second floor, there was another family on the first floor, yet another family on the ground floor, one entrance, one staircase, no private door to the flat. There was no electricity laid on in those days; lighting was by gas. I can remember the gas mantles, quite a good light that gave off, because we didn't know any better. We had no bathroom, the toilet was downstairs and we had to share with another family. For heating we had an open coal fire and for cooking a gas stove. There was the one sink in the living kitchen room and there were two bedrooms. You just lived as you could. The coal was delivered into the cellar, three floors below, and it all had to be brought up by hand, and of course there was no lift. Just imagine the living conditions in the winter! There's the gas stove and gas mantles and a certain amount of gas leaked from them, there's my mother cooking on the stove and the steam coming from any boiling going on, smoke from frying. Then there's the coal fire. The chimney didn't have a very good cowl on it, so any time there was a wind blowing the smoke from the coal fire blew back into the room. Of course my father was sitting there chain smoking. Extremely unhealthy! My mother did somehow manage to get a certain amount of money out of my father on a Friday night after he had been paid before he went out and spent the rest of it at the weekend. We survived!

John Rogers

My Dad

My Dad was born in Back Lane in Brentford. It was a dreary hovel, like you might imagine it to be in Dickens. His name was Albert Alfred Young, but he was always called Tom. On the coke ovens he got very bad asthma from the fumes. He was on the meters and then he was a driver's mate, on the deliveries. He used to carry the heavy gas ovens upstairs on his back. He was never late and never had a day off. He was stone deaf because he'd had a mastoid operation in his twenties and it went wrong, pierced the ear drum, he never had a tooth in his head either. He had seven brothers – they all worked at one time for the Gas Light and Coke Company. All my family did; we got long service awards. My father got killed in 1937, crossing the Great West Road, opposite Beechams. The driver, Captain Philips, was a pilot, driving with no lights, and my father being deaf couldn't hear the car coming. The driver got killed himself in the war a few years later.

Vera Burrows

Sweet Imprisonment

On 21 July 1973, when we boarded the plane at Nairobi Airport, I thought to myself, at last all my problems are now over. The next morning we landed at London Heathrow Airport. The land of England welcomed us, but perhaps the welcome was also tempered with a warning that this was not the end of our problems but the beginning of new more complicated ones which time will present to us.

We lived in Kenya before we came to England. We lived on an island, which was hot but not humid as the cool sea breezes made it quite pleasant. It was a small town and had a small Asian community. There was a spirit of brotherhood among the

The coke gang at the Brentford Gas Light and Coke Company in 1920. Vera's father Tom Young is second from the right, back row.

various sections of the community. For women, life was easy as we had servants to do all the housework.

Why did we come? The political state of East Africa was worsening day by day, more so after the events in Uganda and the expulsion of Asians from that country. People were shaken and felt very insecure. We came to England with our two children who were still in primary schools. Finding rental accommodation became a problem as we did not know where to go or what to do. Many questions were asked by the landlord: how many children we had? how old were they? would there be many guests visiting us? were we from India or Kenya? The last question seemed very odd and hurting to me. We did not know that people living here saw a difference between Asians from Kenya and those from India. In our view we are all Indians.

After a long search we bought our own property. Was this really our own house? I did not like to borrow money at all, it was foreign to me. We were now under a heavy debt for twenty-five years. The term mortgage is equal to 'Mautgage' (meaning 'death' in Punjabi). The worry of the debt took my sleep away.

To find a job was not difficult in those days. I was thankful to my parents for grooming me with a good education. If I was not educated I would have had to suffer in the factories. In the office I was the only Asian and felt the odd one out. I had no problems in speaking, understanding and writing English but found it difficult to cope with the accent. If I was asked to repeat what I had said, I used to think I had said something wrong. I was very self-conscious and could not speak with confidence. During the lunch break I had the problem of what to eat as most of the dishes in the canteen were new to me.

Often I had a feeling of helplessness and an inferiority complex and this hurt my dignity. After some time I got a job in the Civil Service. In Kenya I was in the teaching profession and was a headmistress for two years. I had a lot of respect, status, dignity and recognition for my ability. In my new job I had to deal with the public all day. The swearing and rudeness I encountered was intolerable. I felt that if I was in a similar job in India or Kenya, people would have treated me with utmost respect. Most of my seniors were less educated than me and I resented the subordination in my heart. Because of my helplessness, my mind was reconciled with the situation, but my heart never did. I always felt demeaned, demoralized, humiliated and intimidated.

In this country we started feeling inferior; this complex was created by the attitude of the white people towards us. For example if we were not able to pronounce their names correctly they laughed and mocked us. When they could not say our names they thought our names were strange and funny.

I was quite familiar with the three famous Ws of English life: Weather, Wine and Women. But what I have come across with my experience here is the three Ds: Depression, Diet and Divorce. With the passage of time we have come a long way. We have adapted to the English way of life. Our attitudes, dress, food, way of thinking and even values have changed. Even our names have taken a western flavour; Sudha is now Sue, Harbaus is now Harry, Ungla is Angie, Amita is Amy and I am now Jackie from Jagjit.

Through hard work we are now reasonably financially comfortable and have

Jagjit Chadha in Mombassa, Kenya, in 1973, two months before she came to this country.

acquired many luxuries and comforts of life. However, the question arises: are we really happy and content in our hearts and minds? No, we are not. We do not belong to this country, nor to our homeland. The memories of our loved ones in India torment and haunt us... Yet can we go back and start a new life in India? The answer is an emphatic no! The love for our children and grandchildren holds us back. We are suffering emotionally but are compelled to suffer a life sentence of sweet imprisonment.

Jagjit Chadha

Coal, Coke and the Copper

We lived in Paradise Place, a little row of nine cottages. The rent was 9s a week. The landlady used to come and collect it. She had a big rent book and a black apron with a pocket in the front. My mother used to send me to the door. If we hadn't got the money I'd have to say, 'Could you come back next week for it?' We often got behind with the rent but you could pay a shilling or two off the debt. There was a yard right through the back of the cottages with three outhouses. Three families to one tap and one sink so we had to go across the yard for water. We used to have a stone copper with a lid and a copper stick, you put all your rubbish in the bottom and burnt it to boil up the water for your washing. There was a mangle too. There were three lavatories, just a wooden seat with a bucket, they used to come and collect it. At night we used chamber pots but they had to be emptied. We had no bathroom, nothing like that. When the coalman came he walked right through the house to shoot a sack of coal in the cupboard under the stairs. There was dust everywhere. We had a gas stove with a penny slot meter. No electricity – it was gas lighting. You had to buy the gas mantles, very delicate they were. On Saturdays we used to take a barrow and get a big bag of coke for sixpence from the gas works down by the river. I had to take the wireless accumulator to Mr Goddard; he charged threepence.

Vera Burrows

A Pound a Week

I used to work in the jam factory in Southall. I was on the bench: we had to wash the jars, get all the stuff off the jars, then we used to have to tie 'em down and then we used to have to polish them, you was on piece work then, you never earned a lot of money then. We used to wash the fruit at night. I got married in 1925. Living with my mother, when my son was born, well I had to go to work when he was only a few months old because my husband worked down the market garden. They weren't getting any dole money when they was out of work and when it was wet weather they got nothing, no money at all. Living with my mother that was two pounds a week, if you think back seventy year ago. It doesn't matter if I didn't have the money; I had to find it, because living there, my mother would turn round and say 'Well, you got no money?' Well, you had to pay up. We had two bedrooms where we lived, with two full sized beds, one for the boys and one for the girls. My Mum had eleven children, five girls and six boys, you used to have to lay reverse way. When I got married, my mum put my sister in her room, of course I had the back bedroom. When she got married I turned out of the back bedroom and went in the front room downstairs, but we had no passage there so as you opened the front door you was in your room. So of course I had to do that until my boy was four and a half. Then I went and moved into a cottage one room up and one down, only four doors away from my mum, down the same road. That I didn't mind. I knew very well I could stop out what time I liked.

Cissy Randall

CHAPTER 5

Wartime

John Hearn of Holly Lane, Chiswick, serving in the 20th Bomb Disposal Unit. He is in the centre of the back row, leaning on the van.

First World War

I remember the declaration of war because we had a French governess. We were haymaking one day and a plane came down. A Frenchman; we got him in and he was all right and he met our French governess and he married her. I can remember, at breakfast, her bursting into tears when she heard war was starting. My father was too old to fight in the war but he had lots of responsibilities. I remember his job after an air raid: he had to get on his horse and ride all round Horsenden Hill shouting the all clear. It was the only way to do it. He was out for about two hours shouting the all clear. At the shooting ground we helped develop a shell, about eleven inches long, that punctured zeppelins and set them on fire.

Noel Richmond Watson

Zeppelins

I remember Zeppelins ever so well. I had to run for my life from Zeppelins, they was awful. When we heard the warning we had to run somewhere, my brother dug a hole in the earth for us all to go down when it come. There was a terrible row. We all went down the hole as soon as the sirens go. Down you go and put a board across.

Ada Banks

The War to End all Wars

I lost two brothers in the war and they all kept saying the war was going to end. All of a sudden the church bells were ringing out and I flew up the stairs and put me coat on and ran home to my mother. Everybody was going mad in the streets, kissing one another. I said to my mum, 'Are you going to buy any flags round the corner?'. She said, 'What do I want flags for? They won't bring my boys back.'

Mrs Tunks

A State of War Exists

Then war broke out. I remember on the morning of this, the declaration of war, being at a friend's house; he was the proud possessor of a pinball machine which we'd been playing. I remember it got to lunchtime and I ran home, only to be shushed by everyone seriously huddled around the radio. I remember hearing Chamberlain say the dreaded words. Shortly after this the sirens went. It happened to be a false alarm, but my uncle over-reacted and wanted us all to rush off to the park where deep underground shelters had been prepared. The all-clear sounded before anyone actually did anything. I'm not sure why no one considered the surface shelters that were built in the streets outside the front. They had brick walls and concrete roofs; we did use them later on in the Blitz. I remember the night an incendiary bomb slid from a roof nearby straight into the shelter through the entrance. Father threw it out and dealt with it. He was an ARP warden and spent most nights fire-watching.

Frank Weeden

Gas Masks

It was at school, the gas masks were distributed by a lady who was giving a demonstration on how a gas mask should be put on. Even now I can almost smell that awful pungent rubber smell – dreadful, the claustrophobic feeling as it slid over your head and tied behind with the straps. You had to give a good suck to get the breath in through the nozzle. I was frightened and I'm sure I was close to tears, these things were awful. When she said 'Blow out' the rubber vibrated rapidly and there was a very rude sound, a raspberry noise. It drove the poor lady to distraction!

Roy Bartlett

Enemy Alien

All refugees, all foreigners had to go to a tribunal to establish their credentials. I only had a police registration book which every foreign person had beside their passport and you had to go to the police station every six months to justify your existence.

On 30 October 1939 I was asked to go to the Petty Sessions at Acton Police Court. I had to go before the magistrate. He gave me the title 'Enemy Alien Refugee from Nazi Oppression'. At the beginning I was restricted to within five miles of Ealing. We were four boys; two of the boys lived in Wembley and they went to a different court and they first ended up interned on the Isle of Man. One of the two was sent to Australia, the other was interned in Canada. It was simply luck that I was in Ealing. I was eventually leader of a fire guard and we had the local Forum cinema as an observation platform when the doodlebugs were attacking London. We stood on the roof of the Forum on the platform with a button, which released warnings through the sirens, to say please take cover. At night we watched the flying bombs coming over and when the flame stopped we knew that the bomb was about to come down so we pressed the button for everybody to take shelter.

I got a job at Andrew Frazer's in Hanwell, an engineering company. From

High explosive bomb damage in Talbot Road, Ealing. This is one of the shelters that Frank Weeden describes.

Julius Fletcher with his collection of airgraphs, telegrams which were sent on microfilm by plane during the Second World War.

June to the beginning of the war we were sub-contracting work, which turned out to be parts of the first bombers that were built in the United Kingdom, the Wellington bombers. We were making parts. I worked there right through the war. In those early days, the days of Dunkirk, they needed a new invasion force, so we started rebuilding cylinder blocks for diesel engines that were going to be used in tank landing craft. We did the gang emplacements for the battleships. I remember working on huge hinges, three metres wide. We didn't know what it was all about. We thought the hinges were for some huge building but as it turned out they were for the Mulberry Harbours, the prefabricated

harbours that were eventually used for the allied invasion of France on the Normandy beaches at D-Day. We didn't know about it until after the war because we had a visit from an Admiral of the Fleet, of all people, who came to our premises to thank us for the wonderful work we did.

Julius Fletcher

V2 on Packards

I was a member of the Air Training Corps. One morning a V2 landed on the canteen of Packards Car Company on the Great West Road next to the paint store. I was on my way to school and had my ATC uniform on, and on my way I walked along the cycle track, past Packards. One of the Civil Defence members saw the uniform and said 'Hey, we want you.' I went to Firestones across the road with a trolley and collected sandbags and then I was dragged in. I was digging them out. I was thirteen; I didn't realize the horror of it. Thirty-seven people were killed.

Brian Newton-Cox

Horrendous Sight

It was the Packard Car Company, opposite Gillettes. There was this enormous explosion, even from Southall it was big, and we could see the pall of smoke rising. All of us lads grabbed our bikes and cycled down to see it. I think that was one of the most horrendous sights I ever saw. I shall never forget the rows of bodies lying on the pavement, that is the most horrifying picture that I can ever recall of the whole war. You see the blood, everything, it was a mess.

Roy Bartlett

British Condescension

I was born in Kharagpur, West Bengal where I lived until I came to Ealing in 1948. During the war I worked in the Orderly Room, 91 Air Stores Park, under Squadron Leader Young James, supplying parts for AOGs (aircraft on ground). British officers could be very condescending to anyone who wasn't white. I remember once a flight-lieutenant coming up to me and just

assuming that because I was brown I was also unable to understand English. He pointed to me and said, 'You ... tell ... meee' and then, pointing vaguely somewhere else, 'ord-er-ly room.' Well, because he was an officer I could have been put on a charge for being rude, so I just said in my best English, 'Yes, certainly Sir. Take the second on the left and first on the right and it is directly ahead of you.' He was astonished.

Rita Buckland

Noise

At school in North Ealing, Pitshanger Lane, I became an air-raid warden. They dug up the grass outside and made air-raid shelters. When the sirens went I used to be the last one, conducting everybody in, very pompous and important. You could tell the noise of the enemy, a Dornier or a Heinkel, because they droned. Spitfires had a much more enthusiastic noise. So did anti-aircraft guns on Ealing Common. The noise of a V1 was 'pop pop pop pop pop' and then the silence. And when the silence came you knew it was running out of fuel and going down. From my bedroom in Cleveland Road you could hop to the window and see where – 'putchoo' – they landed. With a V2 there was no warning at all, just a bloody great bang.

Geoff Harper

The First V2 in London

Staveley Road was a V2. Staveley Road in Chiswick was the first V2. I'd joined the Wrens. We'd had a terrible lot of bombing

The Home Guard on Ealing Common.

A V2 bomb exploded at Staveley Road, Chiswick, 8 September 1944, at 6.34 p.m. The following morning the Home Secretary, Herbert Morrison, came down to inspect the crater.

and my father said, 'Why don't you girls get away and get some sleep?' We went up to Nottingham. When my father met us at the station coming back he said, 'There was a frightful explosion on Friday. Everybody's saying it was a gas main. Churchill and all the cabinet came down. There are eight houses down, but nobody's been killed.' Within two or three days the rumours were thick and fast, there had been more explosions and they were certainly not flying gas mains.

Violet Fulford

Indiscriminate Gunfire?

I was cycling along and I heard the roar, the obvious engine note, of a German bomber extraordinarily low. It was coming behind me. I looked round and it was indeed skimming the rooftops and as I got off the bike to dive into the shelter it roared overhead and the rear gunner opened fire. As I threw myself into the shelter I heard the machine gun bullets hitting the road and the rooftops. I can't possibly think that he was firing at me.

Roy Bartlett

Late Air Raid

For night after night, for weeks and weeks and months the sirens had always sounded. If it was 6.30 they were a little late. People used to say, 'They're a bit late tonight, aren't they?' That night nothing happened, no air raid siren. It was deadly quiet and it was a perfect night and I can remember all the people down in the air-raid shelter getting very agitated. There was something wrong: they couldn't go to sleep unless the sirens had gone and a raid was on. It must have crept through to about eleven o'clock in complete silence, then the air raid siren went. Everybody said, 'Thank goodness for that – now we can get some sleep.'

Roy Bartlett

You Kept Going

You kept going. You just kept going, just to spite Hitler!

Dora Wilson

Doodlebug

We were sitting in the sun eating sandwiches and this flying bomb was approaching from the London direction, slightly unusual at Southall because it meant it had passed completely over London. This thing passed very low over the AEC factory and we all relaxed until somebody said, 'Oh Gawd, the bugger's coming back!' It had done a complete U-turn and was flying back on a parallel course. Its fuel would expire any minute. It went overhead and continued towards London, until suddenly it turned again and came back on exactly the same course. It went over the factory again and repeated the manoeuvre a fourth time. It seemed to have some sort of personal commitment to us, but with the engine still going it dived over towards Norwood Green and exploded.

Roy Bartlett

All are prepared for the worst at the Hoover factory in Perivale, 1943.

Hush Hush

Well, in the Home Guard they had a kind of 'scorched earth' policy if the Germans invaded and they were coming this way. This was organized on the borders of Ealing and Wembley. We had certain teams selected then and we had to go out at all times, day and night. They'd come along and say that at such-and-such a time you'll start your run. We were all cyclists of some sort. Some were very keen, others were people who just went to work on bikes but were obviously fairly proficient cyclists. There were six teams, three in each team. We went to Swiftscale at Park Royal, to Summertex, then to Hoovers, Sandersons, Crammick Engineering and also Aladdin. And another place was Alperton Lane where they were making the wings for Mosquito planes, Brown Brothers I think

the factory was originally. There were particular people who knew us. We just had to find these people. They knew us and recognized us. We had to get their signature on a board to prove we'd been. And if there was any danger of the invasion coming this way, we had to go round to them. Then they had to carry out the immobilization of the machinery. This was all more or less 'hush hush'. Even our sergeant said, 'Where do you blokes go? Where do you go every so often?', but we weren't allowed to tell them. I was a corporal in those days.

Dick Adams

Bombed Out

The shop and the house itself were very badly damaged. I think it was about eleven o'clock one night at the height of the Blitz. Dad used to sleep upstairs. I was sound asleep in the shelter. Dad always said he heard the click as the bomb was released. It was then totally obliterated by this crashing Dante's *Inferno* as every window in our house was blown out, the curtains in the kitchen were just one shredded mess. But my sister, her husband and my dad never had a scratch and yet they were all three blown across the room. My first conscious awareness was waking with a pain on the side of my head: the shock wave knocked my head against the brick wall and the whole shelter was filled with a fine grey dust coming in from every nook and cranny and an awful acrid smell and taste. Obviously the bomb was very, very close. There was no panic, tea in fact was being handed round to slake our parched throats; they were very dry and dusty. There was glass and mangled wreckage outside the front door, all our shop

Above: *Dick Adams in the Home Guard.* Below: *Air raid damage in Fisher's Lane, September 1940.*

stock, glass, telephone wires, everything was tangled up on the pavement. The entire row of seven shops had totally and utterly disappeared. My sister always remembers the total silence, apart from the German bomber still groaning overhead; there was a total uncanny silence.

Roy Bartlett

Unexploded Bombs

Once we were completely trained and it was felt we had total confidence in each other, we were put into teams, eight men to a team, we knew instinctively what each others' thoughts and reactions would be. We travelled to all areas of Kent removing bombs and ack-ack shells. When Canterbury was bombed we were kept very busy, working hard from daylight until dark because we could not use lights of any description. At Dover, where the beach was mainly shingle, we once worked for hours waist deep in water to find and remove one bomb. We dug three holes nearly forty feet deep before we located the bomb, which was eventually only six feet below the surface! We cleared bombs in that area for over a year. The shingle was hard, cold and wet and we worked with ropes round our waists as we filled up one heavy bucket after another.

A particular incident I shall never forget occurred one weekend when we suddenly

A team from the 20th Bomb Disposal Unit with a 1,000kg bomb dug up in Kent in 1943. John Hearn is on the right next to the bomb.

Some of the drivers of the Bomb Disposal Gang. John Hearn is on the far left.

had a rush job one. I had applied for leave from Saturday lunchtime until Sunday 2300 hours, but Lt Catt instructed me to help with a job before I could go home. His orders were to pick up some ack-ack shells that had been found somewhere on the surface and were being held by the police. I jumped into the van, which was pre-loaded with sandbags, and drove quickly to the station. I then carefully placed the shells horizontally into the back of the van, using the sandbags to make sure they couldn't move. Lt Catt said I could pick up my pass when the shells were all unloaded so with that in mind I was in a hurry to get the job finished. The shells weighed about 56lb each and, to speed things up, I put one under each arm and jumped off the tail port of the van. As I did, one shell slipped from under my arm and fell to the ground. My heart almost stopped, but I was extremely lucky because although it was one of the shells that should never be tipped forward, for some reason it did not explode. By chance Lt Catt had been looking out of a window and saw what happened. He ran out shouting and his language was atrocious, calling me everything under the sun and saying I should have known better. After I had finished unloading, to calm me down he gave me my pass and told me to get off home but warned me not to do anything so stupid again.

The first time we ever walked onto a minefield on the seashore was nerve-wracking to say the least. When the mines were originally laid they were linked together by wires, but over a period of time

Bomb damage in Duke's Avenue, 19 February 1944.

the sea rusted the wires and they broke. The tide coming in and out then shifted the mines so we never knew exactly where they were and had to hunt for them with mine detectors and extreme caution!

I had another very lucky escape one Sunday morning. Albert, the other driver, was loading up a lorry, a near-side steering GMC, to collect mines that were to be dismantled and destroyed. We had no idea that an undetected mine that had been buried just inside the main gate had moved, and just as Albert drove over it, the front of his lorry was blown off. Shrapnel went right through the petrol tank and into the cab. At first it appeared that Albert was unhurt as no physical injuries were apparent but he

had in fact been totally deafened. Both his eardrums had burst so he had to be discharged from the army. Just an hour or so later I was due to take over the next shift with my lorry to repeat the procedure; my guardian angel must surely have been looking after me that day!

John Hearn

Bomb at Duke's Avenue

The Sunlight Laundry got one. There's a lamp-post and the people was blown up on top of that. They was hanging on it. A lot of people were killed then. We were very lucky nearby. We had no windows. They used to come and board them up. It was in February, I remember my husband had come home that weekend and we were laying in bed. I thought I'm fed up with that shelter. It was dreadful: we used to take our blankets down with us, bring 'em up, take 'em down, because it was damp down there and very cold in the winter. You'd see the searchlights at night. I used to hate that shelter; so that time we was in the house all in one bed. All of a sudden there was such a crash and on the corner by Duke's Avenue, that was bombed completely right along. It shook all our windows out and we shot ourselves out of bed, it was dreadful, dreadful. I had to be brave because of the children. It was terrible, it really was. But really, we come through it all right, didn't we? I never went to work and left me children. My husband used to say, 'When I'm away, don't you dare leave them children.'

Ena Burnett

Stripey

The sirens went and my cat called Stripey came hurtling over the fence, down the garden path, rocketed between our legs and shot into his basket and that was to be his ritual every time the sirens went. They were called moaning minnies. He must have thought, 'That's got to be one hell of a moggie out there!'

Roy Bartlett

Red Cross Parcels

I've seen men sitting there waiting for the white angels. Now the white angels were white trucks with a big red cross on them. As soon as somebody said 'White angels up' everybody would go rushing to the wire, and every man would cheer. And I've seen grown men, tough men, cry when those trucks have appeared, honestly. In my time we was lucky if we got one parcel every three months, but at the beginning of the war they used to get them regular, but seeing that the railways and the roads were badly bombed we would get one about every three months. When you got it, you put it on your lap, and you just sat there looking at it, you was frightened to open it. Honestly, you was frightened to open it. But when you opened it, if it was a British Red Cross parcel or a St John's Ambulance parcel, your best thing in it was a packet of tea. That was the main thing, that was gorgeous. If it was a Canadian one you got a tin of coffee, right. But worst of all if it was a French one, you got coffee but everything stank of garlic. Now when you got your parcel, the four of you would always get together and you would agree as to what to open. One lad would say, 'Well, I'll open my meat today, all right? Then we'll go tomorrow without any, then we'll open yours the next day.' Now the string that tied the box up with, that was carefully cut and you used that to make a mattress with, because your floorboards you had already burnt for fuel, so you strung the string across, all right? Any string left you gave to the theatre company to make wigs with. Now the lids was carefully opened and they was cut, the cardboard was cut into dominoes or playing cards, the lads would cut them up. Any game you wanted they could make, like small chess boards. Any cardboard left was given to the escape committee, if they wanted to make any imitation badges or belts they would melt it down, soften it up, make it like, you know, passe-partout. Now, not one piece of the box or string was ever wasted. One of the biggest

Fred Sims (first on the left) in 1945, a few months after release from Stalag 383, Moosburg, Germany. As Fred says, he'd put a bit of flesh on by then!

treats was, you would get biscuits. You used to soak them overnight, put a few raisins in with them and a little touch of sugar and you would leave it so that it rose to make it come big, then you would cook that a bit on the blower and then that was a treat. Your next treat was chocolate. You got a bar of chocolate so what you did with that, you got an empty tin roughly the size of a shoe polish tin, you put the chocolate in it, and you melted it and waited until it came hard. You would then leave it until it got cold, then each day you would go up to it and you would take just three licks on your tongue. And then the hardest thing was putting the lid back on again, but you learnt control. So you made that near enough last you, with a bit of luck, two weeks, only having three licks a day but that's what you did you know, to make it last. The saddest thing was that in some of the parcels you got prunes and raisins, and some of the lads used to boil these up with the potato peels to try and

make hooch. And we've seen many a lad absolutely in agony, you know. One chap actually died on Christmas morning.

Fred Sims

Books

Chaps were reading books as though they had never read in their lives before. You wrote to the Red Cross. Any book you wanted, dear! It didn't matter what it was. The one thing I will say about being a prisoner of war: you could learn any language that you wanted. I started to... I was going to go out to South Africa after the war with a mate that I met in the prison camp, and I thought that I had better learn Afrikaans. Well I had two lessons and I soon packed it up. Talk about getting a sore throat you know, I packed it up. I mean there were chaps that had never studied say astronomy, they were reading books on that just for something to read. There was chaps there taking university degrees.

Fred Sims

Jerry-baiting

The main activity in the camp was Jerry-baiting. Toward the end of the war they told us not to try to escape, but it's always a prisoner's job to escape. So we thought well anyway we can make it hard on the Germans. Didn't matter what it was, if you could do J.B. – Jerry-baiting – then you did it; you annoyed them as much as you could. You thought of anything, any gimmick; don't matter what it was, you jolly well did it. Water was short, very very short, you see. They'd say water will be turned on eight till nine; nine out of ten times it wasn't. So you would save all the water you could in your little old tin cans, you would hang them up on the beams of a nail. And this Jerry used to come in with his rifle, his bayonet fixed, and then he'd try and get these tins with his bayonet. So we thought, we've got to try and stop him, so he came in this day and hit a couple of tins and nothing happened, and he hit the next one and the whole lot came down on top of him. Well I won't tell you what was in them, very nice. He got the lot. Anyway we was whipped outside, we was taken outside you know, naughty boys.

Fred Sims

Seniority

VJ Day seemed to come out of the blue. We were on AOG [aircraft on ground] duty when suddenly an emergency call came. I answered it not knowing what to expect. A voice commanded, 'What rank are you?' and I replied, 'I'm a Sergeant WAC (1).' He said, 'Well get me someone senior!' So I did, and do you know what the emergency was? The war's over. That was the message, the war's over.

Rita Buckland

Demob and Home

The long-awaited day for my release eventually came and in November 1946, I embarked at Singapore onto a ship called the *Ormond*. Frustratingly, we were delayed for a few days by a cyclonic storm before we could set sail for India. After five days at sea we pulled into Bombay, and then headed home via the Indian Ocean, Suez Canal, Gibraltar and the Bay of Biscay, eventually pulling into Liverpool on Saturday 8 December. I cannot describe how happy I felt to be back in England. Before disembarkation, we were allowed to send a brief telegram home. After queuing for what seemed like hours, I managed to send one to Joyce, saying I would be home sometime the following day. From there we caught a train that agonizingly passed near enough the top of Holly Road, to get to Woking where we were to be demobbed. I knew that like me, Joyce would be counting the hours. We were given our demob clothes – a suit, hat, shoes, tie and underclothes – and the first good meal we'd had in a long time – bacon, sausages, eggs and fresh bread, a smashing breakfast! My mates and I said our farewells, not knowing if we would ever meet again. With all our gear issued we were taken by lorry to Woking station to catch a train to Waterloo and from there we were told to make out own way home. By this time I was well and truly loaded up with baggage! I had all my army gear in a big solid demob box, a kit bag that was packed tight with tinned fruit, a big

Left: *John Hearn*. Right: *Joyce Hearn aged fifteen, in 1936.*

heavy tin box with presents for all the family with cigarettes, clothes (which included a beautiful Chinese-style silk pyjama suit for Mary); all gifts which I had bought in Singapore, and they weighed a ton! When we reached Waterloo, with another chap who lived in Heathfield Terrace, I struggled in quite heavy rain onto a local train that took us to Grove Park Station in Chiswick. I unloaded all my bags and boxes and then carried them in stages to the bus stop outside, from where we caught a no. 55 bus. We had a job to fit everything onto the bus but the conductor was very good, letting us pack it underneath the stairs and wait there with it, saying nothing was too much trouble for soldiers returning from the war. He stopped along Heathfield Terrace for the other chap to get off, then took the bus right to the top of Holly Road and helped me unload all my gear. I shall never forget that day, the rain by then was pouring down so hard is seemed as the heavens had opened up, everywhere looked drab and grey, but to me it looked the most wonderful sight in the world. I was lumbered up with all that luggage and so short of breath that when I got half way down Holly Road, I left the big tin box and the valise in the middle of the pavement and ran down with the rest to knock on the door of No 19. I threw the things down on the doorstep, ran back and picked up the box and valise and as I ran back to the house, there was Joyce – every bit as beautiful as I remembered.

John Hearn

CHAPTER 6

Leisure

Ted Fry, Fred Sherley (crew) and Frank Manning at Southend in 1932. They spent one hour, 12 minutes and 12 seconds with a puncture.

Picnics at the Potomac

The family [the Rothschilds of Gunnersbury Park] used to be in residence only in the summer. I didn't know much about them really. You never asked questions. They were multi-millionaires, the richest people in the world. They all used to come down in their Rolls-Royces: Lord Roper, Lord Lascelles, Lord Derby. Used to have their picnics in the afternoons, with picnic baskets. The chauffeurs used to come and pick them up when they'd finished. They all used to go down to the Potomac in their boats and sunshades, down to the boathouse, all along the water, sunbathing and what have you. As a boy I didn't know what they got up to but since then I put two and two together. Parties on the lawn in the summer, all marquees and umbrellas. If I was walking along and I happened to kick a gravel stone out of the gravel path I used to have to go

The Terrace at Gunnersbury Park.

back, pick it up and put it back. The gravel paths used to be spotless. They had three ladies there kneeling on kneeling pads, hand weeding the paths, with their buckets and barrels. There was never a weed in the gravel paths.

Bernard Collis

The Chiswick Empire

I used to go up there for fourpence, up in the gods, when I was that high. My Dad used to take me when there was people like Max Miller and that. That must have been about 1923.

John Hearn

A Shower of Peanuts

In the thirties we used to pay sixpence and we used to gallop up to get first in the queue to run up – it seemed hundreds of stairs – right the way up and round and then when you got up there you sat on tiers with a little bit of cloth on them. You used to get a bag of peanuts and you sat in the front and threw the shells down on the circle to those posh friends who were sitting down below.

Doris Sands

Oh, it was Brilliant

They used to have some marvellous pantomimes there. I can always remember one they had, *Cinderella,* and the two ugly sisters were Rebnall and West. Do you remember Ethel Rebnall and Gracie West? One was very tall and one very short. And there was always a lovely smell of oranges at that time. Did you know that Larry Adler, the mouth organ man, was at the Chiswick Empire once? He was top of the bill and somebody dared him to go outside as a busker and he got about threepence. They were queuing up to see him but he went outside just playing his mouth organ and everybody ignored him. They had some marvellous names. Just after the war I remember seeing a show with Max Bygraves, Frankie Howerd, Harry Secombe, all just coming out of the Army, the Navy and the forces. You know afterwards they were all such good names but then they had only just come out of the forces. Oh it was brilliant!

Iris Faulkner

A Terrible Night

Do you remember Shirley Bassey? We were in the theatre that night when her husband committed suicide. He flung himself out the window and she came on to the stage and people in the audience were throwing squashed tomatoes and eggs at her. She had to come off the stage because they thought it was her fault, you know, that she might have pushed him out of the window. It was a terrible night, terrible.

Esther Findlay

Buskers

It was wonderful! There were all the old variety artists, Vesta Tilley, the Crazy Gang, Max Miller, Max Wall. Wonderful,

The Chiswick Empire in 1959.

I think, for sixpence. You'd line up outside, because we were all waiting for the cheapest seats, to go into the gods and you went way, way up. Orange peel, nuts, everything went into the circle below, on purpose. A bit of vandalism, I think. If you saw somebody you didn't like, they got it! Yes, it was great! But before we went in, the reason we went an hour early was because the buskers were outside. Now they were worth seeing because there would be these great escape artists. They'd tie themselves up into knots which were locked and bolted and they would get out of them. How they did it I don't know! If you couldn't afford to go in you used to wait outside to see the buskers. They were a treat. Why they pulled it down I don't know. It was a tragedy really.

Vera Burrows

Dressed for Dancing

One and sixpence was quite a lot to go to a dance in those days. You always had a long dress if you could afford it. You'd try and get your hair waved at the hairdressers: iron waved, marcel waved, you know, with the tongs. There were no perms, no make-up, only lipstick. My mother made me a very pretty georgette dress, pea green, and then a pink one. And you'd have dance shoes, black satin or silver.

Katherine Cowper

Long Slinky Dresses

My main interest at that time was ballroom dancing. Quicksteps, foxtrots, waltz, tango, cha-cha. Everybody wanted to be like Ginger Rogers and Fred Astaire. So we would get a dressmaker to run us up a dress. Beautiful flared lace dresses which had to swing out when you swirled around. That was lovely. Mine was always black lace, I don't know why, but I did favour black lace, fully flared. Our best local dance hall was Kew Palais, that was on the bank of the Thames at Kew. The floor was beautiful. In socials and church halls it was just rough wooden floors that you just threw French chalk on to make it slippery. This was a proper dance floor. A shilling and sixpence to go in.

Vera Burrows

Walking Home

The dance finished about eleven o'clock. Sometimes we came home with another girl, it depended if you had a regular boyfriend or not. But we knew a lot of chaps who came from South Ealing and all round you see. One of those would bring me home sometimes. Sometimes we wished they hadn't. You know what I mean? I had an alley by the side of where I lived, Layton Road, and I used to say goodnight to them up the alley, in case my father told me off. I had many a fight up there for my virginity, which I was determined to keep. One night one was so persistent. I knew him too. He was determined. I had to knee him in the you know what to get away, ooh it was a wrestling match!

Katherine Cowper

Dancing Twins

I did ballroom dancing from 1940 to 1967. Waltz, foxtrot, quickstep, tango, paso doble, rumba, samba, jive. I wasn't the right shape for Latin American, you had to be tall and slim. I learnt at the Ealing Academy of Dancing with Dickie Braham. He was about fifty years out of date but I had private lessons with Harry Tucker, who was the bloke who really brought me on at the end. I got all the medals from the Dance Teachers' Association. This picture is of the Southall Ballroom Queen. We're all members of the Fairlawn School, Southall. I'm on the right with my partner, Pamela Cumming. We came third but we should have come second; Pamela was in a rotten temper; her twin sister, Patricia, came second because she was smiling more. The twins lived in Perivale; they really hated each other! The couple who came first are in the centre:

The Southall Ballroom Queen, 1951. Dick Adams is on the far right.

Jacqueline Clarke, unfortunately she was much too short to dance with me.

Dick Adams

Net Petticoats

My mother thought they were terribly frivolous and a waste of money so I made my own. Layers of net, bulky down at the bottom, very scratchy too! Then you starched them so they stood up on their own. No, net petticoats were definitely not approved of! You took them with you in a paper bag and changed in the ladies. I met all my friends in the Hounslow bus garage and caught the 33 bus to the Castle, the big dance hall in Richmond. We sat around at tables, boys on one side, girls on the other, and waited to be asked to dance. Then at half past ten we took our petticoats off

again and caught the bus home. We had to be in well before midnight.

Andrea Cameron

Avoiding Father

My mother and father were very strict. I wasn't allowed out after nine o'clock at night. If we wanted to go up to Chiswick Empire Saturday night, we could go up on our own, first house, but second house we had to take my mum with us. My father wouldn't let us go without my mother was with us. That was as strict as my dad was. Even when I was first married. Sometimes we might miss the eight o'clock bus coming back from Bedfont, so we had to walk, that was over an hour's walk. And if we weren't in at nine o'clock, my father and my mother used to be in bed and the door used to be locked. My dad used to say, 'While you're living under my roof you'll be in by nine o'clock, married or single.' If we see anybody coming along with a pony and trap, my husband used to ask where they were going and that, and they'd give us a lift up and we used to give him half a crown. That was a lot of money. We was sometimes locked out and I'd go 'Mum, mum, would you come and open the door, mum?' My mum would let us in without my dad knowing.

The night before my sister was married she was saying goodnight to her husband-to-be on the doorstep and she was out there a bit too long. My dad goes out there and he says, 'How much longer are you going to be out here?

Andrea Cameron, aged sixteen, in the garden of Auntie Madge's house, Heston, in 1956.

Haven't you had long enough to say goodnight?' My brother-in-law-to-be, he says, 'Oh, well, it's the last night we're single,' and my dad says 'I don't care.' He comes indoors, and of course years ago you had the copper in the scullery, and he went in there and got the copper stick and he ran out the front door and chased him all up the road, shouting 'You haven't got her yet, she's still my daughter.' That was my dad. Mind you he never hit us, wasn't cruel to us. We used to go out at night time and meet the boys at the top of the road and my younger sister would come running down the road shouting 'Dad, she's up the top playing about with the boys,' and he was shouting, 'You tell her she's got to come home.' I'd run down the road behind the house and go round the back and in the back door. I'd see my dad come out the front door and I used to be in bed before he come back in again. And he'd say to my mum, 'Where's Cissy?' And she'd say, 'She's in bed upstairs'.

Cissy Randall

Getting Engaged

We got engaged up there on the platform at the Mayfair Laundry. It was a Wednesday afternoon. So I said to him, 'Anything wrong?' He looked at me, he said 'No, do you think there's anything wrong?' 'Well,' I said, 'look at your face: you're all worked up.' And he said, 'Would you like to see what I bought? Tell me what you think of it.' He got out this solitaire ring. I said, 'Who's that for? What kind of ring is that?' 'Well,' he said, 'it's an engagement ring.' 'Oh gosh,' I said, 'who are you going to get engaged to?' 'You!' he said. 'You're joking!' I said.

Ellen Trent

Wakefields in Chiswick High Road, 1925.

Vera and Harry Burrows, 6 April 1940.

Brentford Football Team, 1932/33.

Wedding Days

We got married on a Boxing Day. And that's another day I'll never forget. The snow was that high they couldn't get us in the church, they had to shovel it away before we could get in. We went to Wakefields to have our photographs taken and they took us and it was so cold. They took us outside ... I was in white, and so bitterly cold. We had our photos taken and they sent the proofs of the bridesmaids and my Fred and me. And when it came to the money, we hadn't the money to buy them so we only had the proofs! We never returned the proofs and that's all I've got! That's all I've got of my wedding, 'cos it was a lot of money back in those days. We never had enough for the photographs.

Violet Brewer

Brentford Football v. Weddings

6 April 1940. That was my wedding day. It was also the cup tie between Arsenal and Brentford. Harry had to come from Chiswick and I had to come from Brentford. 40,000 people went through the turnstiles that day. The whole of Brentford came to a standstill. When Harry saw me he said he didn't know whether to go to the match or marry me. He couldn't get home quick enough to find out the results. I can't remember who won; my mind was on other things!

Vera Burrows

Christmas Day 1936

When I was going to marry my darling here I went to the church down there and we booked up the time to get married. It was sometime about one o'clock. My wife's father was a nutcracker on football for Brentford. I said, 'Well that's it, Dad. I've booked it Christmas Day, one o'clock.' He said, 'You've made a muck up there, son, ain't yer? Brentford's playing at home, kicking off at eleven o'clock.' I says 'I'll go back and see the vicar and tell him to put it back half an hour,' and I did. Brentford kicked off at quarter past eleven on Christmas Day in the morning. I went, we all did – Ethel's father, her brother, my brother, my mate. I had a good shave in the morning, all our things were polished. We come out of the football, trotted home, didn't wait for no buses up to Bush Corner. I could change in about five or six minutes easy, changed into me suit – I got married in a blue suit – ran down the park, they were looking for me coming but I got there in time didn't I and caught yer, didn't I?

Tom Bowles

Chance Encounter

I met my husband on a bike. Yes, I had an accident in the tramlines. I had to pull over for a Boys' Brigade going along. My handlebars got twisted. I pulled it to the kerb and I'm standing there feeling ever such a fool, I was about fifteen or sixteen and I'd got my shorts on and lo and behold two fellas on a tandem came along in plus-fours. I felt so stupid that I was afraid to look up. 'I don't know what's happened to my bike,' I said, and they more or less did it with one finger. These chaps more or less blew on it and put it right for me. That added to my embarrassment. Years later when I was twenty-one I met my husband. He belonged to the Fulham Wheelers Cycling Club. He was the pride of Fulham Wheelers; he was their boy who was going to win all the cups for their club. And we happened to be talking and

Mr and Mrs Howlett with Alan in the sidecar, 1940.

Alan has his own bike. Perhaps Jimmy wishes he does too.

I said, 'Oh, I'm glad they are going to get rid of the tramlines,' and I related the story. He said 'Was it outside the Duke of York, down in Acton?' so I said yes. He said 'Well I remember that, because it was Dave and me.' It was him and his brother. So, I say, I met my husband four or five years before I met him.

Elizabeth Wilkinson

All the Family on a Tandem

We decided to change our single bikes to a tandem. So long as we had our tandem and our sandwiches we were content. We got married in 1936 and still carried on with our cycling. Well, when the first boy came along we bought a Watsonian sidecar to fit on the tandem and then we had another one, so we put the first boy on the back of the tandem and the baby in the sidecar, so there were four of us on the bike. Very often we were stopped by the American GIs. They were amazed and kept taking out photographs. When the boys grew up, the elder boy got a bike of his own and the younger went on the back of the tandem. Then they both got their own bikes; we were on our own again.

Mrs Howlett

Time Trials

This was a twenty-four hour time trial, the Southern Counties 24, closed-circuit road racing. That's what you look like after twenty-four hours of cycling. I'd been 422 miles, 300 yards. You start at one-minute intervals. You're on your own. You start at Hand Cross on the Brighton Road, and go out towards East Grinstead, come back to Hand Cross, across to Horsham, down to Chichester roundabout, in and out of the Witterings, back to Chichester roundabout, down to Havant, near Portsmouth, back to Chichester roundabout, up to the Dial Post on the Worthing Road, which is a sit down and feed place, through to Guildford, Guildford to Windsor, back, Guildford to Esher, back, Guildford back to Horsham and there's a finishing circuit there, about ten miles.

Stanley Knight

Olympic Time Trials

We won all the time trials for two years and then they went and picked four different people. Typical of selectors! This was for the 1936 Olympics in Berlin, the ones which Hitler was determined Germany would win.

Fred Sherley

Long Distance Rides

The first real bike I bought was when I was fourteen. It was a BSA Gold Vase. The cash price was £6 2s 6d but I bought it on the never-never at 2s 9d a week and I had to pay three guineas extra. That was from Retlaws in West Ealing. My friend Sid Carter got a Raleigh Sports Model. We rode thousands and thousands of miles together, to places like Southend, and we came back the same day. The first time we went to Devizes and stayed with his aunt, from there across Salisbury Plain, down to Stonehenge, Amesbury and Salisbury. Then back to Devizes, stayed there and back the next day. About two hundred and ten miles

altogether. We used to stagger into post offices to send a card back home with the time we got there on it to prove we'd been.

He went off to Devizes and back in one day. This was when we were about fifteen. So I thought, well what's a bit further than that? Portsmouth! So I rode to Portsmouth and back. Actually I only had two bottles of Tizer in the saddlebag. I had nothing to eat all day. When I got back I was starving. A few weeks later he went to Bath and back. That's about ninety two miles each way. And I said to him, 'All right, I give in!'

Dick Adams

Sid Carter on his Raleigh, holding Dick Adam's BSA Gold Vase 1935. See the cyclometer.

103

The Milk Race

Cycling was one of my great interests as a pastime and sport, joining the Hounslow Wheelers with brother Ernest, for riding and later racing. When the Feltham Road Club started I was asked to be a vice president and later became president of the club for nine years. In 1958 one of my cycling friends and great organizer, Chas Messenger of Heston, invited me to become a race announcer on the Tour of Britain Cycle Race which he was organizing, being sponsored by the Milk Marketing Board. This appealed to me and I agreed, and for the next eight years my two weeks' annual holiday was spent on the 'tour'. The first one started from Alexandra Palace, and I was introduced to my fellow announcer, one Oscar 'The Duke' Savile: a cigar smoking, sharply dressed character with winkle-picker shoes and slim bow tie, who had taken part in an earlier tour organized by the *Daily Express*. We soon became friends. You could not help liking his somewhat outrageous manner, which certainly helped him along his career. He is better known today as Sir Jimmy Savile. Later the event became well known as the Milk Race.

Eddie Menday

Yellow Kit

Football began to take over my life. We used to kick a ball about, made of rags, in the yard at AEC lunchtimes and then one of the lads came in. He'd found an old pre-war leather football, the old teat bladder variety; he broke his thumbnails trying to stuff it under the lace and it still blew up and held. This was a luxury: we had a real ball. Any excuse for a game, there would be the supervision versus the workers, the factory floor lads versus the staff and then the veterans versus youth. We were just wearing boiler suits and clod-hopping boots. We got a game with the 342 Squadron at the Air Training Corps at Greenford. We played them at Ravenor Park which has so many slopes and angles on it you need one leg shorter than the other to compensate. Kit was a problem, with rationing, of course; clothing coupons in those days were possibly more valuable than money. I managed to scrounge a number of coupons around all my friends and family and got some white shirts. Mum found some yellow dye in the shop, how long it had been there I've no idea, and stuffed them into a big cooking pot and boiled up this horrible soggy, smelly mess. We finished up with this set of canary yellow shirts. It poured with rain and our spirits were pretty soggy as well as we lost 12-0. When we got back to the dressing room, we took the shirts off and found that the dye had run. We were all canary yellow bodied. It took weeks to get off.

Roy Bartlett

Cinema

In the early days in Southall, in the fifties, there were no Sikh temples, no mosques, no Hindu temples, no place for entertainment. There were English films, three cinemas were running at that time, but that was not our language so not everybody could enjoy them. So what we

Gunnersbury Park employees on an outing to the seaside, July 1949. Bernard Collis is on the ground, far right. Eva Smith (Betty Winnett's mother) is in the centre with her hands on her lap. Charles Smith, the horse-keeper, is second from the right of the men at the back.

had to do on behalf of the Indian Workers' Association was, we started renting the private Century cinema, for a reasonable rent. India House were bringing some films from India and were showing them in a cinema in Tottenham Court Road. It was very important because lonely people didn't have any place to go and were wandering around on the streets at the weekends. So we thought it would be a good idea to show the film so that they could get together, talk over their difficulties and problems and have a cup of tea and enjoy the music. That was a very positive thing in those days.

Ajit Rai

Popping into the Matinées

My mother and I were rather naughty: we'd go to the pictures Tuesdays, Thursdays and Saturdays. We'd be shopping in Ealing and we didn't have to say much to each other, we were very close, more like sisters in a way. She used to look at me and I used to look at her and our minds went together, and we'd say 'Now which picture house didn't we go to on Tuesday or Thursday?' and we used to pop into the matinées and get home before Dad came in from work, but he always knew!

Sylvia Middleton

Life Went On Very Sweetly

Before the war, life was always very lighthearted. I worked in the Westminster Bank in the daytime and then was thinking much more about playing tennis in the evening, which was my great thing. But the other thing I was more seriously interested in was taking photographs. I've always had a camera and I joined the local photographic society, which was a very old society in Ealing. I don't think I ever went out without a camera. Saturdays, when the bank didn't work, the thing to do for the young groups of Ealing was to meet in Sayers, the big shop, for coffee on Saturday mornings. All the world and his wife was there. If we went to dances, which we did, there was the Montague Rooms or the Oak Rooms. Ealing had three cinemas, the Palladium, the Walpole, and the Lido. The Lido was in West Ealing and was considered a bit down-market, so we didn't go there. So life went on very sweetly.

Muriel Wodehouse

The Stars

Me and my mother used to go to Ealing Studios and stand around deliberately, to see if we could see all the actors and actresses coming out in their cars. Alec Guinness, Herbert Lom, Jack Hawkins, so many – most of the British film people. We saw Danny La Rue, I remember, very smart, beautifully dressed. Gracie Fields and her husband, Flora Robson, Lawrence Olivier and his wife Vivien Leigh, Joan Collins and her husband Anthony Newley.

Sylvia Middleton

Cranky TV Set

I remember in 1953, the house next door got the first television in the neighbourhood. Like a lot of people they got their first television in really so that they could see the Coronation. I remember everybody crowding into that room to see this cranky little twelve-inch black and white TV set to see the Coronation.

John Rogers

CHAPTER 7

Shops

Shellshear's ironmongers in the 1930s.

Goodbans Department Store

When I first went to Goodbans there were windows rather like an arcade. Everything was displayed on glass shelves and tripods. There were simply hundreds and hundreds of these and they all had to be cleaned with methylated spirits. We had wire models. They had the old wires across the shop that ran all the way across and then down onto the counters. There was an office higher up so the assistant didn't have to worry about the change. She just put the money in this little container and then it used to fly across and then fly back with the change.

Ruby Elvyn

The Cash Railway

A feature of the ground floor was the largest installation in the country of a Lamson Paragon cash railway. There were over 100

Goodbans in 1963.

overhead wires along which were catapulted wooden cups containing cash, into a central cash desk. Two trustworthy cashiers catapulted back change and receipts for purchases. They balanced their books daily to the nearest farthing, one quarter of the old penny. Goods were often priced at, say, instead of 2s, at 1s 11¾d. Customers had the choice of their farthing change or a packet of pins, which cost the traders less. Incidentally the cash railway was the dog's delight as they chased the cups flying overhead.

John Cooper

Pin Money

I can remember going to Goodbans with my grandmother. Whenever she bought anything in the haberdashery that came to say one and elevenpence threefarthings, you would give them a florin and then they used to give you a large piece of paper with loads of pins stuck in lines instead of giving you the farthing change. Pin money!

Doris Sands

Dirty Business

When I first started in the windows there, the first job I learnt was how to curl a coat inside out and pin it underneath so it wouldn't fit. They used to put the coat in the window for a ridiculously cheap price. The customer would come in to try it on. 'I'm sorry, it's far too small for you,

Madam,' because there was far more pin than real thing!

Ruby Elvyn

No Supermarket

It was a beautiful shop down there, that Sainsbury's. You had the two counters, very ornate with marble tops, and they went the length of the shop on both sides. Down the end was a sort of cash place where you went to get your dividend. You got your tea and you queued up for that, and then you got your cheese or your sugar. Next door was the butcher's, all mahogany counters and beautiful tiles. Then you got your greengrocer's and then you went into the chemist next door. So it took a long time to do your shopping.

Sheila Watson

Rabbits and Elephants

Sainsbury's had massive mahogany counters, very ornately carved with marble tops and sawdust on the floor. The butter was cut from large lumps and patted into shape with two wooden pats. Foley's was the greengrocer's. They had a sort of extension which stuck out onto the footpath during the day and was put back inside at night. It was all lit overhead by gas lamps. I remember they used to have covers on them like large broad brimmed hats, like on an ancient warrior or something. And there were rabbits, they hung down vertically and they had their noses in a metal cup to collect the blood dripping down. Where I lived in Baker's Lane there was a greengrocer who had a machine which produced carbonated drinks on demand for a penny. They were served in chipped and scratched bottles, which were used many times. They had a clip on top and you drank from them there and then and handed them back to be used again. We had a barber's and a sweet shop and a rather mysterious shop for us kids which was run by an old chap rather like Steptoe who wore mittens on his hands. He was called Mr Holloway. The shop smelt very dank and musty. I was always impressed by a set of mahogany elephants which stood on the counter, went down in descending size, one huge one and then down and down to a very small one. And tusks.

Frank Weeden

Ice, Eels and Hot Pease Pudding

We used to see the iceman come. You got a bit of that ice and put it in your mouth. He had a big claw, big spiked claw, like a grapple, which he'd dig into the big blocks of ice and he used to chip bits off. You'd pick it up, dirt as well you know, and put it in your mouth, oh it was lovely this bit of ice. We shopped every day because we had no fridges you see, nothing like that. We had a larder with mesh in it to keep things in the air. There's was a butcher's shop up by the church. Bollo Bridge Road was a long road. We had to walk a long way to that shop. At night they would cook saveloys, faggots and hot pease pudding, it was delicious. You'd go up to buy a certain amount and by the time you got home your fingers were in it, scoffing it up and the faggots and the saveloys. Oh it was lovely. With fish and chips you could get a ha'penny and a penn'orth, a ha'penny piece of fish. And we'd

Marks and Spencer, 1934.

extraordinary things. I can remember boxes and cubby holes labelled Black, Lamp Black and Pumice Stone. It was genuine, my Dad always used to tell me; it came from the slopes of Mount Etna. Mum and Dad would really go out of their way, even during wartime when it was difficult, because the customers were their friends; they weren't customers, they were friends. They would go to extraordinary lengths, even after the shop was so terribly damaged by the bomb. We had a young soldier standing outside with fixed bayonet to deter looters, all the shop stock was in complete and utter turmoil. One of our customers brought back an oil stove, which had ended up in her garden. It had its cardboard label, 'Bartlett's Hardware Store' still attached. Dad opened the shop next morning. God knows what he was going to sell.

Roy Bartlett

walk in and ask 'Got any cracklings?' You know, all the bits that fell off the side of the fish were cracklings and that, and he used to put them in newspaper. Everything was wrapped in newspaper. There was a pie and eel shop in Church Road, Acton; pie and mash was sixpence ha'penny. I couldn't afford the eels but my Mum used to buy them. They'd be wriggling in this big bowl. My Dad would kill them with a block and my Mum would gut them, head and tail them. Mashed potato, parsley sauce and eels was a favourite dish of ours.

Elizabeth Wilkinson

Bartlett's Hardware Store

Mum and Dad had a hardware shop in South Ealing. I can always remember it was an Aladdin's cave as a young boy. The most

Where's the Baby?

I can remember when I had my son. I went down the High Street, past Marks and Spencer's, looked at a pair of shoes in Lilley and Skinners, walked in Goodbans and saw some people I knew and started talking. I got right into Woolworths before somebody said to me, 'Did you lose the baby?' and I said, 'No, why?' 'Well, you haven't got it'. I said 'No, he's outside Lilley and Skinners.' He must have been there for a good half an hour. The pram was still there, the shopping was in the bit underneath.

Doris Sands

Stockwell's the Chemist

I remember Mr and Mrs Stockwell and their son. They all served in the shop. It was a typical

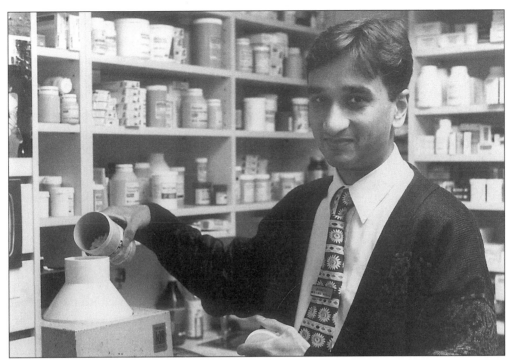

Raj Patel in Acton Lane, 1999.

old English chemist's shop. The outside was painted dark green. And the son Mr Stockwell, the young man, did all the heavy loading and he helped his mum and dad, which I thought was very nice. Everything you could possibly want in toiletry was in Stockwell's lovely shop. Actually they became friends of mine. They had time, even Mr Justin, to ask you about yourself and your family. Mrs Stockwell took care of the ladies when they wanted advice and Mr Stockwell spoke to the gentlemen; old fashioned but lovely.

Rita Buckland

All the Family

I've been here in Acton Lane for five years. I named the shop Alisha after my seven-year-old daughter. My wife Anisha sometimes helps behind the counter and my four-year-old son Ravi sometimes entertains the customers.

Raj Patel

An Exclusive Shop

There was a beautiful dress shop in the parade, and Hall's on the other side. Thomas Hall, on the corner just past the church, a beautiful, exclusive shop where you bought blouses and underwear and gloves. Tommy Hall's – you only went there if you could afford to buy their gloves or underwear or their beautiful blouses. They were very exclusive. And Mr Hall would greet you at the door. I can remember

having my gloves fitted to me on my hand –
where do you get that done nowadays? And
they had glove stretchers, which were like
hair tongs, to stretch them, because most of
them were soft leather.

Sybilla Skelton

Brawn, Kippers, Coffee and Spices

Keeping food in the shop was a problem,
especially in the hot weather. My father had
a big icebox with shelves, and at the top was
a cradle. Two or three times a week the ice
people from Fulham would come round with
a horse-drawn cart with pieces of ice about a
foot thick. The cradle would be taken out
and the ice dropped in. It would be carried

in on a dirty sack. That was the only way in
the summer months to keep meat
reasonably fresh. You see families then
would have a cool box hanging outside their
window sills, and many a time people would
say to my father, 'That brawn thing you sold
me went into jelly,' and my father said, 'Yes,
and where did you keep it? In a hot room?
I'm sorry, I can't do anything about it.'
Brawn was the biggest headache of all – it's
cooked meat made from the pig's head.
There was very little refrigeration in those
days. Cheese you didn't worry about; you
never kept cheese in the fridge like you do
today, because cheese matured naturally,
coming in big wheels, or halves, and you
would see where the taster had been put in,
and it would be green. Now Sayers the
fishmonger, they would always have a
beautiful display, but it would be all ice,
chips of ice. They used to smoke their own
kippers and haddocks. You've got the baker's
shops, baking their bread, all on the
premises. They had their bakehouses,
beautiful. Then there was Cullen's the
grocers: when they were roasting the coffee,
oh, the smell was wonderful! They had all
the little boxes with the different spices and
herbs. Shopping was an exploration in those
days.

Sybilla Skelton

The Bike Shop

I spent all my growing time living above the
shop, quite a small area above and I was
interested enough to decide to come into
the business when I left Ealing Grammar
School. I came to work with my father and
the one thing with the business at that time
was my father had run the shop for what he

*Roger Woolsey outside his bike shop in Acton
Lane, 1999.*

referred to as the chaps with the workaday bike. After Augener's [the music printing factory] packed up, the factory was taken over by the Wilkinson Sword factory and most of the fellows who worked on the production line rode bicycles and that kept my father and myself in the beginnings very busy. We had a period where cycling fell out of fashion: it developed what is known as the cloth cap image at the time, about the mid-sixties, and all the working chaps were aspiring to sort of better forms of transport. So to fit in with that, I came up with the idea – sort of after discussion with me Dad who had a love of these bikes – to diversify into selling mopeds as well as bicycles. It was lucky we did because that turned out to be the fortune of the shop. If we'd tried to stay purely with bicycles, as turned out with a lot of bike shops at the time, it would have finally floundered during that period, but I'm pleased to say we saw that through and here we are now with cycling very much back in fashion. People are delighted with their bicycles and the shop is continuing to go from strength to strength at the moment. My whole life is involved in the world of cycling, both during all working hours and all my spare time as well. My wife sort of says that if it hasn't got two wheels and a pedal on it, then things aren't of too much interest to me.

Roger Woolsey

Milk and a dash

Wasn't there a cake shop in the High Street, called Zeta's? You always went to Ealing Broadway for quality. If you wanted nice cakes you went into Zeta's. Mind you, if you went into Joe Lyon's you could have – what did they call it? – milk and a dash! That was very milky coffee. I mean that was a highlight. You actually had a cup of coffee outside your house. It was a treat. A very modest one. When we were out shopping my mother would say, 'I know, I'll take you into Joe Lyon's and we'll have a milk and a dash.' It was in a glass with a metal holder. I'll always remember this. But the public toilets! They were rather frowned on by my parents. If you were desperate you could use them but it was not considered to be a desirable thing. You didn't know who used them or what you might catch!

Viv Holding

Galloway's

Shops have changed hugely, as you would expect. There was a beautiful butcher's shop, an open butcher's shop opposite Turnham Green, which offered every summer to the cricket team a flitch of bacon or a ham to anybody who could hit a cricket ball into the shop. I can't imagine how anybody was allowed to hit cricket balls over the road into the shop but that's how the story goes. Up the High Road there was a shop belonging to Galloway's. It was a perfect shop for children because they had every single toy you could think of: they had an enormous number of lead farm animals, which I used to collect. I had two pennies a week pocket money (in the late 1920s) and I used to save it up to buy another thing for my farm. It was my most precious possession. There were all sorts of wonderful things you could buy if you had a great deal of money, like tumbrils with horses to draw them. Galloway's was an extraordinary shop because you were allowed to walk around

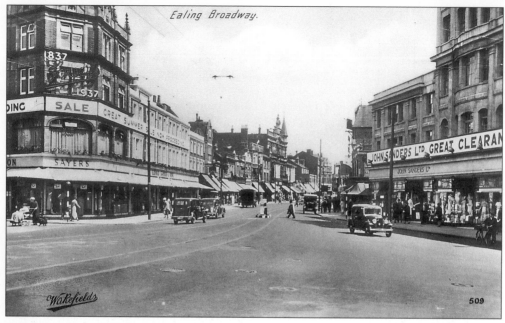

Ealing Broadway, 1937.

without buying anything. They didn't mind children going round and round the shop; the children were all beautifully well behaved. I have to say in those days nobody pinched anything and they certainly didn't knock anything over and they were absolutely charming, gentle people. They were there all my childhood until my own children were old enough to go and buy things at Galloway's. It was terribly well known in Chiswick; it was the place to go and buy things if you were a child. There was Dent's across the road and Dent's was a hardware shop and it had the most beautiful smell. It was a mixture of turps and oil and all that sort of thing, and I just loved going in there. I can remember my mother used to go shopping every day. We used to walk down to the shops and I'd say, 'We're going to Dent's, aren't we?' and she'd say, 'Not today.' My heart would sink that we were not going to smell that lovely smell. At Cullen's we would sit on high stools at the counter and my mother would read out her shopping list and she would decide on what we were going to buy; of course, we didn't take anything home with us, we just walked home and then in the evening a boy came on a bicycle and he would deliver everything in cardboard boxes and we never had to carry anything about.

Gwyneth Cole

CHAPTER 8

Events and Places

Police at an anti-National Front demonstration in Southall 1979, which led to a riot.

Death of PC Kelly

It was six o'clock in the morning. This was 1919. Mr Randall, the kitchen gardener and myself were going to work. We were walking to the park from Acton Town station and we were stopped by two detectives: had we seen anybody? There'd been a robbery in the Acton town booking office and it appeared that he had broke into there and he'd run right up to the park. There used to be six big elm trees,

very very old elm trees, and it appeared that this burglar run up there and hid himself behind these trees. PC Kelly had run up after him, blowing his police whistle and Mr Cleaver, who was the gatekeeper to the Rothschilds, he come running down with his dog, shouting, and this robber shot Mr Cleaver in the arm and he chased this robber. While Mr Cleaver was running down to the trees he shot PC Kelly in the eyes; shot and killed him. Mr Cleaver chased him up to the park and he

Gunnersbury House in the early 1920s. Mr Gilbert, one of the tree-moving team, remembered that they were always 'tree shifting'.

run over to the Baron's Pond outside, over into Napiers and into Ealing Common and he disappeared and they never did find him. This man was put on identification parade and Mr Cleaver said he was sure he could pick him out but he was that kind...

Bernard Collis

Seeing the Rothschilds

I was eleven, about 1922. I did a paper round. I worked for W.H. Smith's, at Acton Town station. I used to come to Gunnersbury House. I used to deliver a morning paper and the *Evening Standard* at night. My first introduction here was in the winter. My first walk down that drive was driving me mad,

because there was gas lights. I used to dread coming in here because there used to be dogs roaming about. It was a most frightening experience walking down that drive, pitch dark. To me, at that age, it was terrible. I remember it was on a Saturday morning when the coach came out and they, Mr and Mrs Rothschild, were in it. Drove out the main gate towards Ealing. Massive coach drawn by two horses, beautiful – to me it was, anyway.

George Joel

Opening of Gunnersbury Park

1926: everything was spick and span and tidied up and all the seats and tables were put out on the North Lawn in front of the mansion. It was all laid out for the grand opening, opened by Neville Chamberlain. Miss Smee was there, she was a mayoress of Acton, a magistrate and the first woman who looked after the museum.

Bernard Collis

Gunnersbury Park

I remember the opening of Gunnersbury Park. I listened to Chamberlain's speech. I do remember there were two police sergeants from Ealing, doing jujitsu. One was a footpad. Everybody was dressed in their best. In 1926 any woman of any standing who had a fox fur would wear it, summer or winter. Chamberlain was in frock coat and tails. My sisters wouldn't go out without gloves, mother would wear a hat and father always a collar and tie. Gunnersbury Park was very popular at the weekends, there would be a stream of people coming up Bollo Lane. Gunnersbury Lane was a very narrow country lane: you had to squeeze against the park wall to let a pony and trap pass. There was still a farm there – I remember the sheep and the shepherd. We used to call the Lionel Road side Fifty Acre Field. In the early thirties Cobham's had an air circus there. You went up for five shillings in an aeroplane, a biplane. It took about four to six passengers. Alan Cobham's

Gunnersbury Park was opened to the public on 26 May 1926 by Neville Chamberlain.

Left: *Ena Burnett, aged twenty. She was born 1910.* Right: *Ena's daughter Doreen, born in 1932.*

air circus. It was fourpence for half an hour on the boat pond. The park was very well kept with its flower beds and stately trees. No walking on the grass, it never occurred to you.

Dennis Bowen

Smiths Crisps

When my daughter was a baby in the pram, I used to walk up the Great West Road – there wasn't a building in sight. There was nothing there. All there was was crisps. It wasn't a factory, it was just like a big galvanized place. It was never like it was. How they did the crisps in there I don't

know. I used to walk all the length of the Great West Road and come back with her in the pram.

Ena Burnett

The Boat Race

One of the things they were selling along Chiswick High Road were favours for the boat race. There would be big black velvet coloured boards on a pole, which the people trying to sell them held up. The favours were incredibly elaborate and quite expensive. They were made of crossed oars of bamboo and painted with the right colour, Cambridge or Oxford stripes and little pieces of ribbon to match, tied together. There were all sorts of things like fluffy creatures, navy blue or pale blue, they came out many weeks before the boat race. The schools wouldn't talk of anything else except the boat race, whether we were going to be cheering on Cambridge or Oxford. I had to cheer on Cambridge, because I had a boyfriend there, ten years older than me. It was a bit difficult finding your best friend was Oxford, you felt very antagonistic to her which was terrible. The boat race was an enormously exciting occasion. I don't think there was space anywhere all the way along the river from one end of the race to the other. We always went to the Chiswick Bridge end where we could watch the boats come in and also see the boats taken out of the river and taken to the boat house. On the other side in Barnes there was a huge high brewery building and on the top there was a pole with a pivoted pole across the top and from the pivot were two balls, one pale blue and one dark blue on bits of rope. I expect they were manipulated by a man who could see the course from the top of the building. When the Oxford boat was in the lead up went their bobble and down went the Cambridge one and *vice versa* and this was incredibly exciting. It doesn't sound very exciting but it was. Then when you saw the bobble creeping up again and Cambridge was getting nearer to being level with Oxford, goodness me the excitement and the cheering that went on. Behind the two boats there were vast numbers of police boats and river steamers. All the steamers came out on that day and were following

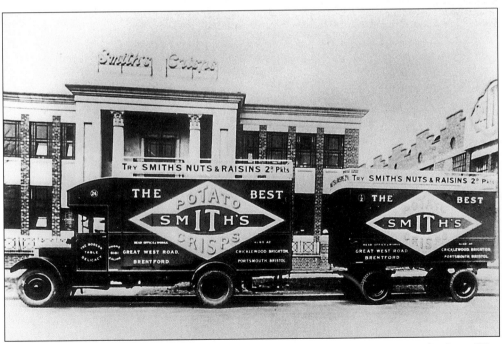

The Smiths Crisps factory in the 1930s. Smiths was one of the first firms to move to the Great West Road, in a single-storey factory in 1927. Ena Burnett must have seen it just before they built this larger factory.

Marion Wenbourne and friends dressed as Bavarian girls for the Lord Mayor's Show, 1938.

and there was an enormous wash which used to splash everybody.

Gwyneth Cole

Lord Mayor's Show

We were in the Federation of Working Girls' Clubs and we belonged to the keep fit class. In 1938, the last year before the war, we were in the Lord Mayor's Show and our girls were dressed as German Bavarians. Press photographers kept asking us to 'Smile please' or 'Just do that bit of dancing again will you'. It was a very exciting day; the directors (of the Cherry Blossom Factory) gave us the day off. We had to go for training some weeks beforehand. We marched behind the Metropolitan Police Band up to the Guildhall. Then we started off on the route, marching and dance steps, dancing forward in time to the music played by the police band. The pavements were packed with people cheering us on, some of them shouted for the 'Lambeth Walk' and 'Knees Up Mother Brown'! We had lunch of Bovril sandwiches and Horlicks and Ovaltine.

Marion Wenbourne

Smog

The fogs were really dreadful, it was eerie you know. Really thick and really dense. It had a weird effect on you. You just felt as if you were in another world, sort of thing. Everything seemed far off. The traffic was going so slow, you could walk quicker than what a car could move, the fog was so dense. Sound was sort of muted. They say people used to wander off and fall in the river. Motorists always had somebody walking in front of them with a white handkerchief to keep them on the road. They couldn't see the pavement or anything.

Elizabeth Yates

Oswald Mosley

I remember Lady Mosley. She was very nice and she let me go and borrow the books that Oswald Mosley had as a boy, and I read them all. Mosley was first of all our MP there. He then turned into that Blackshirt business. I remember him in the village hall. I remember a meeting, we all went along and when he got up my father who was in the front row got up and started going for him. Mosley said, 'I'll come down and knock your block off!' When he said that nearly half the back of the hall stood up and said 'You dare try!'

Noel Richmond Watson

VE Day Street Party

They started collecting for the street victory party, Wedmore Road, Greenford, long before the end of the war. It never occurred to us that we might not win. Our mums were asked to save ration book points. On the morning of VE Day the men strung up lots of Union Jacks and bunting and put up some trestle tables and benches for the party. Us lads built a massive bonfire outside no. 25. We got a

bit carried away and by the time we finished it was about twelve feet high. We all dressed up for the party. I was thirteen and had just got my first pair of long trousers, so I wore them. Somebody made up some paper hats with V on them but I wouldn't wear one. After the party a photographer came and took a picture, the first photo of any of us for six years. We had races and games for kids and grown-ups. One mum won a race but unfortunately the boys holding the finishing line didn't let go when she finished and she came down a real cropper. It was a really hot day and they put some benches on the pavement under a big rowan tree, which was in this bloke's front garden, so that the old folks could sit in the shade. He came out and made them take the benches away. Nobody ever spoke to him again. When the bonfire was lit it really went up, we thought we might have to call the fire brigade. It gave off a ferocious heat. We put potatoes in, they came out like charcoal but we still tried to eat them. The council got the street gas lamps going. When they came on we could hardly believe it after six years of blackout and torches. We rushed indoors and came out with comics and stood around the lamp post laughing at the fact that we could actually read them. Mr Saville, the scrap merchant at no. 33, brought a piano out into the street. He sat down and played anything we wanted by ear. We sang all the wartime songs, 'Roll out the Barrel', 'Run Rabbit', 'White Cliffs of Dover', 'We'll Meet Again' and so on – and people danced. Then we did the hokey-cokey and the conga up and down the road. It was a great atmosphere. Us lads kept putting more stuff on the fire to keep it going. I think it finished about

A VE Day street party in Wedmore Road, Greenford, 8 May 1945. John Cordon is the sixth from the left, middle row.

midnight. I was still so excited I couldn't sleep. I kept getting up and looking out at the glowing embers of the fire, only a few yards from my window. The next morning it was just a pile of ashes. It had burnt off all the tarmac on the road, the council came and patched it up but you could still see the scar for years and years after.

John Cordon

Armistice Day

The war memorial stood on Ealing Green, near the library. I remember when it was November 11, Armistice Day. We crowded round the memorial and hymns were sung, remembering all the soldiers of both world wars that died. The two minutes' silence affected us all very much, more so then because the war was not so long over. I was thinking of all the friends in the RAF who flew over and never came back. And that was a very sad moment for us, even Fred, because he lost a friend. It was happy in one way that we could still continue to remember the people we knew so well but it was also sad that they never came back. I remember my Dad switching the radio on, we had one of those old fashioned radios, and he stood to attention and encouraged us to respect the dead. And he was praying for his friends in World War One and I was praying for my friends in World War Two. Nobody was forgotten. The traffic stopped and there was silence everywhere, in the shops, everywhere. It all seems to have stopped as the years go by.

Rita Buckland

Riots in Southall

In the sixties and early seventies the police were very unfair, in the sense they wouldn't listen to the youth. They were very rough with them, they would beat them, mistreat them in the police stations, and the youth would fight back, even assault the police, and then came the tension between the police and the youth. We were the people who wanted to keep the peace because that was in our favour; we didn't want to create tension, we didn't want to create conflict. The Indian Workers' Association played a very vital role in keeping community race relations.

In 1979 the National Front was holding a meeting in the Southall town hall and the police were determined to teach us a lesson that we should never again do this thing, so they brought in three to four thousand police into Southall. In other parts of the country at the time the councils were advised by the police not to allow the National Front to hold meetings and they were cancelled, but not in Southall. We protested against the council decision not to cancel the booking. It was a premeditated thing to teach us a lesson.

I was in the front. Every coloured person, irrespective of whether he was indulging in violence or not, was beaten by the police, on horses, indiscriminately; everybody was beaten and there were more than one thousand Asians who were injured. Blair Peach was a very decent person, from New Zealand, a teacher; he was simply dedicated against Nazism, Fascism, so he participated against the National Front meeting and he was taken by the SPD people eventually, and he died. Blair Peach died a noble death and we should respect him. He was not fighting in the police, he was not a member of the Labour party, he was not a member of

The police at an anti-National Front demonstration in Southall in 1979.

Southall riot.

the Tory party, he was a teacher and he gave his life for a very noble cause and he must be remembered all the time.

Ajit Rai

I Like it Here

31 July 1963 I came here. I was living with my cousin in Hounslow and I got a job at London airport. Sometimes we were called Paki, but we are not from Pakistan, we are from India: we are Sikhs. We are Sikhs, so why not call us Sikhs? It hurt when people called us Paki. or you blackie, go back to India, things like that. It hurt me, no doubt about it. If people from the British community had gone to my country I would respect them, you know. But this was only momentary. Attitudes towards Indian people have changed; relationships between different cultures and races have improved so much, you know; everybody now mixes with everybody else. I don't see myself as Indian so much as British. I like it here, we are very happy, I have good friends, people here are very nice. My children are highly educated here; I am very proud of them.

Harnam Singh

A Ghost and a Mummified Cat

I left Russia in June 1918, when I was eight. We went to Estonia, just over the border and very near St Petersburg, where we had some property, some factories. We just crossed the border. My father decided that we could not possibly receive a decent education there so we decided to go to France. We went by way of England and we were going to stay for a fortnight but we found that it was such a pleasant country with such pleasant people that we decided to stay. We lived near Barons Court. I went to Kensington High School for Girls, the first two forms were co-ed. I couldn't speak a word of English; I felt very uncomfortable I must say, dumb as a fish. We came to Chiswick in 1975. The rates had shot up in Golders Green where we were and we were looking for a smaller house. April found an advertisement for an old cottage in Chiswick and it was the right price, £20,000. I knew Chiswick because my father's brother had been living there for some time after the war. He had founded a house in Blenheim Road for old indigent Russians who came after 1917 and April had been asked to organize and run it.

We saw the house, no 2 Arlington Cottages, in torrential rain; we practically had to swim through the garden but we fell in love with it. It's a very, very old house, very ancient, full of charm. There's a Roman floor under the dining room. Roman troops came and camped on the green and the commander had his house built here. In 1720 they tarted it up and rendered it into its present shape and form. The House of Arlington, the bailiff. Now it's divided into three cottages. Three old girls lived here right up to the 1960s. I

Arlington Cottages, Chiswick.

Silver Jubilee party in Chandos Avenue, 1977. Jim O'Connor is on the far left.

believe it was a charity thing. We found it very pleasant living here. But when my sight went and after April died, I simply couldn't live in it by myself, so as you know it's up for sale. Do you want to know about the ghost? There's only a ground floor and a first floor and the architect we bought the house from thought there might be something between the ceiling and the roof so he pierced the ceiling and out fell a small piece of paper, rolled up. On it was written in eighteenth century writing 'I must not speak in French class'. Then we found a dead cat, mummified. It had died of starvation and had been put there in the first quarter of the nineteenth century to ward off ghosts. Isn't that odd? A ghost appeared to a friend of ours one

night, stood at the bottom of his bed and grinned at him, he said he was terrified.

Kyril Zinovieff

Queen's Silver Jubilee

Everyone in the street was willing to donate £2 per person for the Silver Jubilee street party. The street was blocked off and people moved their cars. Canopy across the road, lots of bunting, fancy dress, races, conjuring tricks and magic, sit-down tea. We had a huge cake decorated with a Union Jack with Chandos Avenue in letters down the centre. In the evening there was a disco and a bar with home brewed beer, very popular then. It was the best party I had ever been to, the atmosphere was great and we had a lovely balmy evening.

Jim O'Connor

Concorde

I've lived in this area thirty odd years – the aeroplane noise! I absolutely dread Terminal Five being built because I live directly under the flightpath. It's quite impossible in the summer to hold a conversation, stopping every thirty seconds for a plane to go over. And at least twice a day when Concorde comes over, the whole house shudders. Once a chunk of solidified urine fell into someone's garden near here.

Anne Neville

Wind and Weather

Do you remember 1976? There was a long drought, lots of subsidence to houses in the road. You could feel the tension in the air until the weather broke. When it at last started to rain, people came out of their houses and stood in doorways to watch the rain. You could feel the relief. The storms of 1987 – I've never known wind like it. Our back door was smashed

The Firestone Tyre and Rubber Company Factory, Great West Road, Brentford, 1928.

The Firestone factory was demolished in August 1982.

open with the force of the wind and all the glass was smashed. Trees were blown down, roofs of houses were damaged.

Jim and Sally O'Connor

Demolition of Firestone's

Whitsun Bank Holiday my daughter told me that as she came along the Great West Road she noticed that there were cranes with large iron balls round the Firestone Building. This could only mean one thing. So all day we actually witnessed the destruction of the building. Everything was bulldozed to the ground. I wanted one of the tiles with the Firestone emblem on it as a souvenir of all the years that I had

spent in the engineering department there. The man couldn't remove it without breaking it.

E.G. Bartlett